2.45

Campus Power Struggle

*Trans-*action Books

Campus Power Struggle

Edited by
HOWARD S. BECKER

Trans-action Books

Published and distributed by
Aldine Publishing Company

The essays in this book originally appeared
in *Trans-action* Magazine

TA Book-1
Library of Congress Catalog Number: 78-96124

Contents

Preface

However diverse their attitudes and interpretations may sometimes be, social scientists are now entering a period of shared realization that the United States—both at home and abroad—has entered a crucial period of transition. Indeed, the much burdened word "crisis" has now become a commonplace among black militants, Wall Street lawyers, housewives, and even professional politicians.

For the past six years, *Trans*-action magazine has dedicated itself to the task of reporting the strains and conflicts within the American system. But the magazine has done more than this. It has pioneered in social programs for changing the society, offered the kind of analysis that has permanently restructured the terms of the "dialogue" between peoples and publics, and offered the sort of prognosis that makes for real alterations in social and political policies directly affecting our lives.

The work done in the pages of *Trans*-action has crossed

disciplinary boundaries. This represents much more than simple cross-disciplinary "team efforts." It embodies rather a recognition that the social world cannot be easily carved into neat academic disciplines. That, indeed, the study of the experience of blacks in American ghettos, or the manifold uses and abuses of agencies of law enforcement, or the sorts of overseas policies that lead to the celebration of some dictatorships and the condemnation of others, can best be examined from many viewpoints and from the vantage points of many disciplines.

This series of books clearly demonstrates the superiority of starting with real world problems and searching out practical solutions, over the zealous guardianship of professional boundaries. Indeed, it is precisely this approach that has elicited enthusiastic support from leading American social scientists for this new and dynamic series of books.

The demands upon scholarship and scientific judgment are particularly stringent, for no one has been untouched by the current situation. Each essay republished in these volumes bears the imprint of the author's attempt to communicate his own experience of the crisis. Yet, despite the sense of urgency these papers exhibit, the editors feel that many have withstood the test of time, and match in durable interest the best of available social science literature. This collection of *Trans*-action articles, then, attempts to address itself to immediate issues without violating the basic insights derived from the classical literature in the various fields of social science.

The subject matter of these books concerns social changes that have aroused the long-standing needs and present-day anxieties of us all. These changes are in organizational life styles, concepts of human ability and intelligence, changing patterns of norms and morals, the relationship of social conditions to physical and biological environments, and in the status of social science with national policy making.

This has been a decade of dissident minorities, massive shifts in norms of social conduct, population explosions and urban expansions, and vast realignments between nations of the world. The social scientists involved as editors and authors of this *Trans*-action series have gone beyond observation of these critical areas, and have entered into the vital and difficult tasks of explanation and interpretation. They have defined issues in a way making solutions possible. They have provided answers as well as asked the right questions. Thus, this series should be conceived as the first collection dedicated not to the highlighting of social problems alone, but to establishing guidelines for social solutions based on the social sciences.

THE EDITORS
Trans-action

The Struggle
For Power on the Campus

HOWARD S. BECKER

So many colleges and universities have had their confrontation, so many unlikely ones, that we can now take it that whatever school has not been so favored soon will be. North, South, East and West, black, white and mixed, private and public, Protestant, Catholic, Jewish and secular, male, female and co-ed—however we classify colleges, every type has been hit. That suggests very strongly that whatever is going on represents the outcropping of some force or circumstance found in colleges generally. Who could object to the suggestion? Even if we identify that general set of circumstances, as I propose to, as a shift in power relationships among the major participants in college life, the result is still a social scientist's platitude, useful for guiding further discussion but hardly controversial.

If, however, you utter that platitude to anyone personally involved in a campus uprising, it loses its obvious correctness. "No," they say, "You don't understand. It's different

1

here." And so it is. The pieces contained in this volume make clear, among other things, just how different colleges and their discontents can be. The issues differ: racism, free speech, faculty involvement in war research, the impact of the college on the neighborhood, drug use, personnel policies, and so on. The active participants differ: in some places a small group of activists, in others, thousands of "ordinary students"; in some places the faculty has been involved more than others, the administration has played quite different roles in various places, the outside community's influence has varied. The results differ greatly: some campuses settled matters quickly, others saw bloody and long-continuing internal war.

I want to try to make clear how it is the same everywhere and yet everywhere different. Briefly, it—the causes and character of campus disorder—consists, as I have said, of a change in the distribution of power among the people who act together to make up the college community. Matters regarded as settled unsettle themselves. Students want a hand in governing themselves, in choosing their teachers and curricula. Faculty, where they do not have it, demand more of a say about campus rules and procedures. Administrators find their established prerogatives threatened, as do some faculty and students. The "haves" fear to lose what they have had; the "have-nots" hope to gain what they have not had; both take such measures as seem to them feasible and available, given their resources of time, energy, allies, will and tactical advantage. When one group questions hitherto accepted allocations of power, the event encourages others to do the same, making it seem that revolution is upon us.

At the same time, colleges differ in the way power has been allocated and exercised in them. Some faculties have a very strong voice, others none at all. Some administrators have involved students in community decisions, others have not. Some campuses have paid more attention to local residents than others. Every campus has found its natural balance point—the point at which everyone has enough of what he wants that he doesn't feel, at the moment, like doing what he thinks necessary to get more.

I don't imply, in speaking of a balance point, that the accommodation so arrived at is more than temporary, for it obviously shifts when the elements involved change. Nor do I imply that people are happy with their lot; they may be very unhappy, yet fear that their power position affords them no way to ensure change or that what they would have to do to provoke change would cost them a great deal in other ways. Nor do I argue that the accommodation or balance actually struck represents some optimum or that this mechanism guarantees that everyone will get what they deserve. What is optimal depends on who it is supposed to be optimal for, and such pluralistic balancing ensures that people get what they "deserve" only if we believe that people deserve only what they are willing to sacrifice for. If we have some other notion of deservingness—if, for example, we believe (as I do) that people have some rights of autonomy and self-determination by virtue of being citizens and human beings—the balance that arises out of power considerations will often be unjust.

In any event, what different classes of participants want will vary from place to place; what they would actually have to do to get it, and what they think they would have to do, vary as well; what they fear to lose differs. That is why participants assure the generalizing analyst that "it is different here." It is different, in the particulars at stake and in the tactical and strategic considerations involved. But some generalizations can be made as well.

Before suggesting a few of those generalizations, I want

to comment on the kind of public attention current campus troubles have received. Newspapers and television have treated them conventionally: as instances of exciting trouble. Reporters do not, therefore, give the details necessary for a workable understanding of what has occurred in any particular event. They give what has become conventional for that class of story: what "demands" were made; what indignities administrators suffered; whether the police were called; how many were arrested; did anything "new" happen or was the standard script followed. They do not explain the underlying power situation that provoked the incident and conditioned its outcome. More important, they give scant coverage to matters settled peacefully. When black students carry rifles at Cornell, every paper carries the picture. When Northwestern settles its troubles with black students amicably, the media concentrate on a "new" demand, for separate housing. This makes it difficult to arrive, by comparison, at an understanding of what causes the trouble. Finally, the media do not cover at all those matters in which people exercise power covertly, as when, for example, campus psychiatric services provide "intelligence" to administrators.

News of campus troubles provokes commentary from one and all, most especially from outraged professors and administrators. The commentary typically asks *why* students have suddenly started to act outrageously and answers by postulating some clearly irrational motives and psychological processes. Thus, one commentator traces current difficulties to student needs to show their independence of their elders. Another thinks it arises from a new and fallacious belief among youth that we can now provide plenty of everything for everybody; when they discover the hard fact that we cannot, they have tantrums. Many criticize students for ignoring such "natural" allies as the labor movement and the Old Left, for failing to see how their "counterproductive" tactics make things worse, for having no positive program, for being politically and generally ignorant, for being the dupes of devoted revolutionaries who don't mind destroying the university in an effort to change society.

What the question and all these answers accomplish is to focus attention on the students, to make their activity problematic. But we cannot understand a complex event involving many groups by analyzing the origins of the behavior of one of them. Even if the analyses were correct, which I judge they are not, we would still require similar knowledge of the other participants and of the sequence of events by which all those kinds of people interacted to produce all the events that actually occurred. The papers in this volume for the most part provide a more complete analysis; where they do not, it is because they have focused on a group ordinarily ignored, like the college psychiatrist or the right-wing activist. Taken together, they allow us to make some tentative general statements. Like others, I will for convenience speak of students as a monolithic "they." But we should not forget that students come in many varieties, whose differences help explain the current ferment.

The troubles have been building for a long time, at least since the end of World War II when the college population began to swell with the increasing proportion of the college-age group who went to college. The change. in numbers, and the change in the kinds of people recruited as students and faculty, broke down existing accommodative patterns on many campuses. Veterans refused to wear beanies and abide by other hallowed campus traditions which new faculty and administrators were just as glad to give up. Faculty, whose bargaining position improved with every jump in the college population and in available research funds, refused to accept what they now came to see as an ill-paid, subservient and degraded position. They demanded and got better. Well-established patterns of cooperation between deans and presidents, on the one hand, and campus leaders in the student government and in the informal consortia of fraternities that often ran them, on the other, eroded as student numbers increased beyond what that system could successfully contain. Faculty and administration involvement in defense research angered students whose politics questioned the morality of that research. None of these things happened in a day. Together, they produced a situation in which a lot of people were unhappy about a lot of things.

Even those most critical of student movements concede the difficulties and inequities in existing arrangements. But why, many ask, do They have to be so violent about it? Why can't They play by the rules of the game we have always found workable? We can approach this in at least two ways. We can question the viability of a system in which some people never win. We can also suggest that the matters at issue involve fundamental status realignments that those in power will not willingly contemplate, changes they can prevent becoming issues under the existing rules of the game.

Organizations, colleges included, depend on the continued assent of all their participants for their continuing ability to operate. Participants give their assent when they believe that they are getting something they want out of that participation, when they know of no better place to get it, when they do not feel free (because of loyalty or coercive pressure) to withdraw their participation. In the absence of these conditions they may simply withdraw from the organization; faculty often express their dissatisfaction that way, especially when market conditions favor them. If enough people withdraw, the organization must, however distasteful it finds the prospect, change its practices or else find new recruits. I have never heard greater frustration than that of the president of a small sectarian college, who found the competition of a newly-built state college so great that he dared not act on his philosophy that education was a privilege, not a right. He could not throw out students demanding more power on campus; enough had already moved down the road to the new campus to make his financial position very shaky.

Ordinarily, participants do not withdraw. They convince themselves that, while they will not get all they want, they will get enough of it enough of the time to make it worth staying on. You can see the advantage of staying in an organization that allows you to win some of the disagreements you get into. College students very often have conceived of their position this way. Did the Dean refuse to budge on the issue of drinking in the houses? Yes, but he gave in on parietals. Did the administration deny our request for pass-fail grading? Yes, but they let us invite whatever speakers we want. Win a little, lose a little.

But times change, and what students once settled for as winning often enough no longer seems sufficient. The reasons for this have to do both with the changing nature of youth—its independence and discontent with a society and government many of whose actions seem prima facie exploitative and crazily self-defeating (*Catch 22* expressing the mood perfectly)—and with the increasingly difficult conditions of college life. The increase in numbers, the separation of the faculty from the campus community, the increasingly disorganized or, better, unorganized state of the student body, have made things worse for students. They no longer have much influence over the conditions of their lives, these being increasingly set by more pressing constraints of budget, personnel and the diverse pressures Clark Kerr described in *The Uses of the University*. They no longer win here and lose there. In fact, they find it hard to find out where the fight is, as everyone explains how "it is out of our hands" and "nothing can be done about it."

Under these circumstances, students conceive of themselves as never winning—never winning anything they are really interested in, anyway. The game may be played according to the old rules impeccably, but those who never win begin to believe it is not worth playing. They think about changing the rules in a way that will make the results more satisfactory. That is one answer to the question of why current confrontations take the form they do.

The other answer deals with the tenacity with which those who now run universities have held on to existing power arrangements, for it is that tenacity which has convinced students that they have no chance of ever winning anything worth winning under present circumstances. What do the grown-ups fear to lose, that they are willing to go to these lengths to defend?

Let me begin the answer with an observation made by Irving Louis Horowitz during the 1968 Stanford sit-in. Students invited faculty members into the occupied building to discuss things with them. But when faculty members entered, students addressed them, no doubt with some trepidation, by their first names. Whereupon many of the faculty, unable to bear that indignity, left without the discussion they had come for. Similarly, it is reported that Mark Rudd scandalized the Columbia faculty by saying "bullshit" to them. (Plenty of other faculty had already been turned off by the slogan, "Up Against The Wall, Motherfucker!") The general charge that student demonstrators lack civility has been made repeatedly, and the implication has often been drawn that this is no small matter, that it rather represents a fundamental departure from the norms of civilized conduct and that the barbarians are therefore already inside the gate.

Faculty and administrative reaction to these indignities seems extreme, if the actions are taken at face value. All these people have been called by their first names before, and have heard those obscenities before. But, of course, they react not to the immediate event but to what it symbolizes. It symbolizes, in a way that would seem trivial if it were not for the reaction, students' intention to overturn the existing hierarchy of academic life, a hierarchy that distributes quite unequally participants' power over one another. In the conventional college, faculty and administration make rules for students to follow: rules governing when they will engage in what academic pursuits and for how long, rules governing their personal lives and habits (who they will sleep with and where, which drugs they may take and which not), rules governing political activity. Administrators may enforce these rules lightly, selectively or not at all, but they regard them as theirs to make and enforce. They do not propose to allow students to have any say over the conditions of faculty and administration work and life; the thought that students should regulate *their* academic pursuits, personal habits or political activities is bizarre on its face. When I speak of hierarchy in academic life, I refer to this asymmetry in the power to make legitimate rules for others, an asymmetry student actions threaten to upset.

People who occupy a favored position in a hierarchical system generally justify their position by their superior knowledge of its operations and ethos, by their superior and lengthier commitment to it, and by appeal to the traditional wisdom of mankind. Many faculty and administrators so justify their asymmetrical power over students. They perceive the conventional courtesies students ordinarily accord them as an appropriate recognition of the legitimacy of hierarchical difference and of the justifications on which it rests. They likewise perceive the ritual discourtesies students have been offering them (as students no doubt intended they should) as a declaration of war on the hierarchy and the justifications it rests on.

As they should, for etiquette and civility always consist of the peaceful recognition of status relations. Having good manners means to keep to one's place of superiority, inferiority or equality with grace and a good spirit. Violations of the rules of etiquette signify a deliberate intention to move out of one's place as when, in the old days, a Southern Negro refused to step off the sidewalk to make way for a white.

Take first names. Americans ordinarily use first names as speakers of Romance languages use second person pronouns. A Spaniard says *tu* to intimates and equals, in which case they reciprocate, and to servants and children, who however address him as *usted*. We similarly first-name our equals reciprocally, and our subordinates asymmetrically. When a student first-names a professor without permission, he serves notice that he regards himself as an equal, as would a servant who said *tu*.

But if students regard themselves as the equals of the grown-ups, where will they stop? What privileges will they not demand? What existing privileges will they not interfere with? These matters worry academics, even as they admit that there are inequities. Yes, of course some professors are bad teachers; of course, a few are neurotic or sadistic, a few are incompetent and some spend too much time consulting. Still, by and large the system works well; most teachers are honest, decent, competent and hard-working. We put up with the others—as long as they have tenure—because that is the price we are willing to pay for the protections of academic freedom. While I more or less accept that conventional view, I also know that it is mostly students who have to pay that price. I do not have to sit through boring classes conducted by incompetents, or put up with the sadistic use of grades or neurotic classroom displays. But students sometimes do. If promotions and tenure were in student hands, what would that do to the careful system of bargains, alliances and accommodations by which faculties presently survive? What would happen to our protections against external interference? Would students start telling me what or how to teach? Could I stand to work under such a regime?

The questions are serious, and no new accommodation can be reached which does not include recognition of the rights without which faculty will not willingly continue teaching and will start looking for other work. Nevertheless, any new accommodation will doubtless include some fundamental revisions of the status differences symbolized by the current violations of civility. Students will probably not get to tell professors what to do. More likely professors will simply stop telling students what to do, leaving much more freedom of choice for everyone. The battle cry is "Student Power," but the result I expect and hope for is a freer system of Less Power. But the privileged give way reluctantly, and students have discovered that the only way to make their demands heard is to violate etiquette and break out of the game as it has been played up till now. We need not, however, take their current incivility as a mark of congenital and incurable barbarism, but rather as a tactic that will be succeeded by a new civility appropriate to the new balance that will eventually be reached.

I have spoken as though every member of the campus community has already chosen his side, and as though there were only two sides. In fact, although moments of crisis produce polarizations in which that extreme is approached, a characterization based on dramatic confrontations hides an important feature of the current troubles. Many are not aligned, including many faculty and probably a large majority of students, and much of what occurs during crises consists of a struggle for the allegiance of the uncommitted. When student strikes succeed, it is usually because they have won that allegiance. An administrator may believe his just cause allows him to call in the police, but the move alienates those whose support he needs unless he convinces them that his cause is indeed just. Their enlistment on the other side, or even their careful cool neutrality, undoes him. He needs more from his constituency than "A plague on both your houses," an increasingly common reaction of "typical" students. When student actions fail, it is because they fail to convince that same majority that the immediate issues reflect a basic illegitimacy in the institutions of the university. This occurs both in the case of activist rightists and in left-oriented campaigns that fall flat, as many unpublicized ones have.

Another element in the situation has barely begun to assert itself. Universities have always depended on residents of the surrounding community for cooperation, however passive, in the school's operation. The cooperation may consist of no more than a tacit agreement not to vandalize school buildings or assault students and staff. We realize how important that minimum is when residents start to withhold it, as they have in the vicinity of many urban schools. Now couple this with residents' growing awareness of the way colleges destroy existing neighborhoods as they expand, of the way college expansion (like many urban renewal programs) serves to clean Puerto Ricans, blacks and other "undesirables" out and thus "improve," at least from a realtor's perspective, the area. Residents, sensing their ability to make trouble and thus be heard, understanding now that they have something they want heard, more and more play a part in campus crises, throwing their support most often to black students or to students generally. Other elements in the community donate their support less directly, by tacitly supporting the use of police and troops. In any event, community residents worried the Columbia administration, appeared on the San Francisco State campus, created Berkeley's People's Park, and sat in themselves in the administration building of Chicago's McCormick Theological Seminary, where they demanded low-income housing in the immediate area.

The articles in this volume embody various of the concerns and arguments I have expressed. No one volume can do more than sample the vast area that needs to be covered, and I have chosen articles that emphasize variety. Gusfield describes the basic changes in American universities, and we then proceed to three of the most celebrated confrontations: Columbia, San Francisco State and Cornell. Simon and Carey describe one of the early difficulties over the racial question and Schiff introduces us to the activists of the Right. My own article considers the politics of campus drug incidents, and Szasz discusses the political uses of college psychiatric services. We conclude with Hochschild's description of the quite different way of organizing university life that has come to pass in present-day Cuba.

Northwestern University   *Howard S. Becker*
Evanston, Illinois

Beyond Berkeley

JOSEPH GUSFIELD

After a decade in which college students were condemned by their elders for sins of apathy and docility (they were called "the silent generation"), the recent strike and riots at the University of California in Berkeley mark the beginning of a new period of student action in American universities. Most observers of the Berkeley events agreed that more was involved than the specific political issue of student rights to organize. A major source of discontent stemmed from the feelings and fears which students have developed about the character and purposes of American universities in the past decade. These discontents and their sources are not unique to Berkeley. They are the common characteristics of most big universities in the current American academic system. Because they are common to many colleges and universities, we can expect that the California riots are only the beginning of a coming movement for educational reform led by American students.

Much discussion of the genesis of student hostility to administration and faculty has singled out a villain—the "mass university," sometimes called the "multiversity." In my analysis of American universities, the issue is more complex than that of organization type. Bigness is only one thing that has happened to colleges and universities in recent years. Other changes have contributed even more crucially to the development of confusion, fear, and distrust in student attitudes toward education and educators.

The dramatic increase in college attendance in the past decade bears witness to the very high regard that Americans have for college education. In the midst of all this noise, there is still room for some small concern about where this big push toward college may be taking us as a culture and as a nation. There is room for concern about the effects of the college experience on the goals and values of students.

Several years ago Philip Jacob in a book called *Changing Values in College* suggested that college did not have much impact on student goals and values. He found that neither teacher nor subject matter seemed to affect the general drive toward material success that dominated the student's conception of education. Some small elite colleges like Wesleyan and Reed, Jacob found, did have impact upon student character. Student bodies at such colleges showed considerable change toward a liberal, antiauthoritarian set of values. This was far from the case at most schools and especially at the large, mass educational institutions supported by public funds where changes were less often observed.

Despite best seller, legend, and movie portrayal, these small elite colleges are not the typical campus of the 1960s. The transition from the small elite liberal arts college to the large mass university and the implications of the change for student life is my major theme. Over the past several decades, and especially since World War II, a series of contradictory forces have upset the isolation of American colleges. These forces are in the process of creating a new sort of college environment, with important consequences for the kinds of life choices that confront college students.

There are four processes involved in this transition. The first is mass education—the change in the character of the student population recruited, and in its size. The second is the remarkable change in the size and functions of modern universities. The third is the change in the faculty itself—from the locally attached college teacher to the cosmopolitan professional oriented to a world of research and specialized disciplines and less oriented to the world of the students. The fourth point, which is in itself a summarization of the effects of the other three, is the change from the aristocratic cultivation of persons to the meritocratic training of personnel.

The impact of meritocratic training is, to me, far and away the most important part of the whole scene. The transition from aristocratic cultivation to meritocratic education is occurring just when the economic base of our society makes aristocratic cultivation possible on a larger scale and minimizes the meritocratic functions. This is one of the biggest sources of student confusion in contemporary American universities.

If this discussion appears overly critical of present American colleges, it is intended to perform the role of "devil's advocate." There is much that American colleges and universities do very well, much better than they have ever done. There is much that is salutary in the trends referred to here. But the purpose of this essay is neither to bury nor to praise but to raise issues.

The first great change in American college education

is the shift away from aristocratic recruitment toward mass recruitment. By aristocratic recruitment I mean the recruitment of a small percentage of the society, based largely upon income and social background or exceptional talent. College has ceased to be aristocratic, the privilege of the few, and is instead becoming the expected experience of many. We have almost approached the period in American society when you can say that there is a college for everyone and everyone for a college.

In 1910 approximately 67 out of every 1000 persons aged 18 entered college. In 1939 about 14 percent of the 18 to 21 year olds were enrolled in a college or university. By 1961 that percentage had increased to 38 percent. After 1970 we expect to get about 50 percent. A 1959 survey showed that nearly 70 percent of children under twelve were expected to go to college by their parents. College is no longer the area of a few of the rich, the well-born, or the extremely talented but is instead becoming the normal experience of a majority of young people in the United States. Large percentages of the present college population are "first generation," the first of their families to go to college.

This great growth in college entry is not only a matter of a greatly increased population but of a fundamental shift in our conception of who can go to college and who ought to go to college. It is a result of many forces. Our economy is more professionalized then ever before. In 1960 for the first time in the United States we had more professionals and semi-professionals in the work force than farmers. Our research and records-oriented economy needs white collar and technical employees. Our affluent society can afford leisure and education. Our equalitarian values demand that this valuable commodity be widely shared. One possible result of this push toward college could be an increased selectivity, where American universities take in many but also throw out those who fail to meet the tests. This does not seem to be the case, however. Studies tend to show the enormous persistence of students and the sheer difficulty of throwing them out. Like the cat, they come back. If they don't get a degree in the institution where they started, they may well get one somewhere else. Our estimates now tend to look as if two-thirds to three-quarters of the students that enter college do get a degree, somewhere, sometime. It is no longer true that the lower middle classes and the families of skilled workers are under-represented in the American college population. It is still the case, although decreasingly so, that the children of un-skilled and semi-skilled workers have not been motivated into college in large numbers.

As we continue to recruit ever large numbers of college students from lower social levels than have gone to college heretofore, college becomes *the* basic social divider in our society. In many ways the criterion of college education is more revealing for behavior, attitudes, and opinions than the occupational distinctions which have preoccupied sociologists in the past.

A second factor of change in American higher education is the fundamental change in the nature of the institutions that provide it. Increasingly the model of an institution of higher learning is a large university (10,000 to 20,000 students and even more), state supported and comprehensive, urban, and both graduate and undergraduate. In 1951, American private colleges enrolled over half of the American college population. Since then, public universities, including junior colleges, have absorbed over three-quarters of the enrollment increase; public universities now account for over 60 percent of the total college student body. In 1960 over 40 percent of the students enrolled in the almost 2000 American colleges and universities were enrolled in 143 universities. Sixty of these 143 universities have over 10,000 students, and nearly half of them are publicly controlled. It is here, in the large state university, that the basic trends of American education are forming.

The typical state university offers a bewildering array of courses. These can range from viticulture to microbiology, from advertising to astrophysics. Clark Kerr, president of the University of California, has come to refer to the university of today as a "multiversity" because of his response to its highly disparate curricula. Dr. Kerr should certainly know, since he heads an organization whose diversity and internal conflicts are perhaps matched only by the American government. What the multiversity means, among other things, is that the liberal arts curriculum is no longer the center of a college education. It means that the assumption that all students who have been to college have a basic education in common no longer holds. More than half the bachelors' degrees granted in the United States in recent years have been in the areas of engineering, commerce, and education. Less than 25 percent of the students take degrees in the liberal arts (assuming that these might be called a general education).

Growth in size and complexity is what many refer to as the development of the "mass university." Large classes, vast dormitories, complex organizational rules, and the impersonality of faculty and administration are a far cry from the student and teacher sitting at opposite ends of a log and exchanging ideas. In an atmosphere of bigness the student becomes his records and the teacher becomes his examinations.

Students of the giant multiversity are not likely to develop strong, sentimental ties to *alma mater*. They are unlikely to think of the institution they attend in those terms

quences for the functions of a college education, especially the mythical liberal arts function of the college. The idea of a meritocracy was developed by Michael Young, a British sociologist, in his recent book, *The Rise of Meritocracy*. The contrast, of course, is with aristocracy. The meritocracy is a society in which social position and economic position are gained on the basis of merit. There is complete equality of opportunity; positions are allocated on the basis of talent and performance rather than inheritance or social advantage. In this society, the educational system is the basic institution that attempts to sort and select personnel. In such a social system, students are pressured toward a career orientation very early in their college careers. The university's own internal organization into departments, schools, and majors makes it necessary for the student to make up his mind early. Until he does, he will feel that there is some inadequacy both in himself and in his education.

The student in this system is terribly afraid of making mistakes; his fear permeates his relationship with the new, terribly distant figures of judgment and hell-fire, the faculty. College administrators are always telling students to avoid concentrating on grades, but they all recognize that the truth is otherwise; the grade is of immense importance in a meritocratic system of learning where vocation and future are of crucial importance to highly mobile students. There is little room in the life of the student for making intellectual mistakes, for taking courses which may not be related to a future.

The rise of meritocratic education represents some immense gains for our society—gains for a democratic value system as well as for an enlarged pool of trained manpower. I do not suggest that we can or should abandon these gains. I do want to take a look back at the traditional, liberal arts college of the aristocracy, to appraise the particular value it had for society and to see what, if anything, we have lost with its passing.

When very few went to college, and when college entrance was largely determined by income and social position to begin with, the preparation of students did not stress future economic roles. Choice of curriculum and performance in college were not crucial to individual students. The faculty could be ignored with impunity.

One consequence of the college of aristocracy was, of course, what I call the *low play* rah-rah model of the American campus so dear to the heart of Hollywood. But the college of aristocracy also offered another possibility, an orientation to *high play*, to intellectual fun and games. The *high play* model of higher education sees college less as a preparation for the future and more as a period of isolation in which it is possible for students to try on different identities by a process of experiment and vicarious experience in order to decide where their eventual values will lie. The role of liberal arts has been precisely this: to provide that kind of distance toward his life that comes once in the lifetime of a student when he is detached from home and community. This is the only time when he is free to play with ideas without being strongly limited by his future. This process of identity play meant that college was a period of value choice and experiment, intellectually as well as emotionally.

The isolation and lack of seriousness of the liberal arts college could permit a degree of playfulness which is at the center of intellectual pursuit in the ideal of the liberal arts. Arthur Miller has perhaps made the best single characterization of *high play*. Writing about the new repertory theatre in *The New York Times* Miller said, "I have felt it destructive to the imagination of all concerned that all esthetic innovation and risk should be instantly transformed into a financial risk. The word 'play' means, at least in part, a playfulness. It is hard to play in a defensive, cautious, psychological position." It is precisely this defensiveness and caution that is increasing among multiversity students.

It is at this point in my analysis that meritocracy must be seen as resting on a myth. It is the myth that economic demands are producing the huge increases in college enrollments. While there are significant increases in technology which necessitate highly educated personnel, these are not sufficient to explain the high levels of student populations. More to the point, our economy is so automated and mechanized as to produce abundance with smaller percentages of unskilled and semi-skilled workers. So college students could not be absorbed into the economy if they were thrown on the job market immediately after high school. What is happening in American life is not only an increase in technical needs but an upgrading of many jobs to require college graduates solely because college trained people are available. The increased enrollment in college creates its demand as much as it responds to demand.

It is significant that in the Berkeley riots the student group least active was the one most open to the impersonality and bigness of the multiversity—the engineering, science, and technical students. Such students seemingly know where they are going. (Although when they get there they may find their knowledge obsolescent or their tasks far more routine and detailed than they had imagined.) A great many students in American colleges and universities do not know where they are going and have neither past capability nor institutional support for the leisurely pursuit of aristocratic education.

In an abundant economy, not only can we afford a college for everyone but we need the consumption of such leisure. The student knows that he must go to college if he is to get "a good job," but he is wise enough not to see much relation between what he does there and any specific job. He knows that a college degree is a certification that he has played the game of grades and rules adequately. Even in the technical areas, general scientific education is beginning to supersede specific training for a specialty. Lacking the capacity for *low play* of previous college populations, our present students are too Puritanical to approach their education in a spirit of *high play*.

Their confusion is a reflection of their plight in an economy which makes it possible for Everyman to be an aristocrat. Their vague sense that college has not turned out to be either intellectually exciting or vocationally meaningful is a part of their discontent. Playing the game of grades is both farcical and dangerous when you don't hold any of the cards. Healthy human beings are likely to stand this alienation but not everywhere and not forever.

I don't know how we can graft this function of providing "play-time" onto the meritocratic university. Mass education, the multiversity, the weakening of faculty and student ties to particular institutions—all work against it. But I do know that the truly creative intelligence needs this play-space for its proper growth.

Despite a certain danger implicit in much student action, the Berkeley riots have had a valuable effect on American colleges. In frightening administrators they are leading them to look at "the human equation" in the classroom. In making students on other campuses more explicit and more active about their discontents they are demonstrating that "systems" may not be so inevitable. Even professors are beginning to wonder what their students think.

March/April 1965

Columbia: The Dynamics Of a Student Revolution

ELLEN KAY TRIMBERGER

The student demonstrations at Columbia University in the spring of 1968 caused a very serious institutional crisis—involving the disruption of the university for two months, the arrest of more than 800 students, the injuring of almost 250 students and faculty, and the prospect of continuing conflict. To explain why, one must first understand how the institutional weakness of the university and the politicization of students in recent years led to confrontations between students and the administration.

Starting in 1966, students resorted to direct action against the administration to protest against university policies toward the community and its cooperation with the military, the C.I.A., and the Selective Service. The administrators responded first with concessions, and later with repression, but they failed to re-examine their basic policies—or to make any reforms in the way the university's policies were determined. In fact, the public policies of the university (as opposed to its internal academic issues) were being decided by only a few administrators, after little or no consultation with the faculty, let alone the students.

This combination of a remote and unaccountable administration, a politicized and dissatisfied group of students, and a virtually powerless faculty was explosive. Add to it the unhappiness of the faculty and students over the declining educational quality and reputation of a great university, as well as the absence of effective ways to seek change, and you have a highly overdetermined "revolutionary" situation. (A survey by Allen Barton—"Student and Faculty Response to the Columbia Crisis," Bureau of Applied Social Research, Columbia University, June 1968—found a strong link between student and faculty dissatisfaction with the university and their support of the demonstrators. Thus, 57 percent of the most-dissatisfied faculty and 56 percent of the most-dissatisfied students thought that the sit-ins were justified, compared with only 12 percent of the most-satisfied faculty and 30 percent of the most-satisfied students. In the university as a whole, only 66 percent of the students and only 58 percent of the faculty were satisfied wih Columbia's educational quality.)

For more than 20 years two extremely weak presidents have ruled Columbia, with little contact and rapport with faculty and students. Since the retirement of President Nicholas Murray Butler in 1945 until very recently, Columbia's administration had also been very decentralized. Each school and division had a good deal of academic and administrative autonomy, even to the extent of raising its own funds. What this meant was that the core of the university—the undergraduate colleges and the graduate faculties in arts and sciences —declined, both financially and in educational quality. The pay scales and the teaching loads of these faculties did not stay in line with those of other major universities, and the educational ratings of many of Columbia's famous departments dropped (surveys by Hayward Keniston of the University of Pennsylvania, 1957, and the American Council on Education, 1966).

Several years ago, the Columbia administration launched a massive campaign to stem the university's decline. Their reform plan called for a centralized fund drive, as well as for the physical expansion of the university into Morningside Heights. But these plans for expansion brought Columbia into conflict with the residents of the neighborhood, with city and state officials, and with Harlem leaders (Harlem is next to Morningside Heights, and its residents especially objected to Columbia's plans to build a gymnasium in an adjoining park). Thus Columbia, like other metropolitan universities, was drawn into the urban crisis. But because of its stagnation for the past 20 years, even in construction and in fund-raising, Columbia was in more desperate straits than most other universities, and its officers and trustees were more likely to think not of the public's needs but of the university's narrow self-interest.

At the same time, Columbia students were becoming more and more involved in social-action work with the poor who surround the university. (Since 1966, the largest and most active student organization has been the Citizenship Council, whose 1100 members take part in a variety of community-action projects.) The students' work with the poor brought them into direct opposition to the administration's community policies. Even more important, many students were politicized by the Vietnam war, and became antagonized by the university's contribution to military research.

The students, however, lacked effective channels within the university to express their discontent and to influence administration policy. Student structures are weak at Columbia, and those organizations that have tried to use legitimate channels to reach the administration usually have failed. In Columbia College, the students voted more than six years ago to abolish the student government. The all-university student council is not respected by most students, primarily because it is so powerless. For example, its resolutions in the past two years—on class ranks for the draft, military recruiting on campus, indoor demonstrations, the gym in Morningside Park, and the tuition increase—had no influence on administration policy. Nor did the administration formally or informally consult the student council. In fact, several months before the demonstrations both the president and vice-president of the student council resigned, saying that it was completely ineffective.

Moreover, students were unable to get effective faculty support for their grievances, because of the weakness of faculty organization. At Columbia there is no faculty government. The university council is composed of two elected faculty members from each school, the deans, and a number of administrators, but it is chaired and run by the administration; it meets only three times a year; and it deals almost exclusively with technical and routine matters. Of the arts and sciences faculties, only the small faculty of Columbia College has a formally constituted body that meets often and sometimes takes stands on policy matters. In recent years, a few active and concerned faculty members have used regular committees, or set up ad-hoc ones, to investigate controversial subjects with policy implications. But their reports (in 1967, on student affairs, on reporting class ranks to draft boards, on university civil-rights policies, and on faculty housing) generally were disregarded by the administration. Last year a member of the only standing committee of the university faculty admitted in public that his committee had very little power, and charged: "The present system of government at Columbia is similar to that of Tsar Nicholas II."

Faced with an unresponsive administration and a powerless faculty, student activists turned to direct action. In 1966 and 1967, a coalition of moderate and radical student leaders, with wide undergraduate support, won important concessions from the administration after mass demonstrations and threats to strike. These concessions included:

■ a university policy of withholding class ranks from the draft boards;

■ the establishment of a special tripartite commission (student, faculty, and administration) to try students who had demonstrated against the C.I.A. Most students saw such a judicial commission as setting a precedent toward greater due process, and as moving away from the traditional methods of student discipline at Columbia, where students were accused, judged, and punished by the dean's office.

■ The cancellation of army recruiting on campus and of the annual Naval Reserve Officers Training Corps ceremony.

At the end of the school year in 1967, the student newspaper, *The Columbia Spectator,* wrote (March 17):

"Within the last 12 months, student organizations—enjoying the general sympathy of the student body as a whole—made demands on the university which are of unprecedented nature. And, in turn, the university has given unprecedented response to these demands. The confrontation between the two has developed into what may be a revolution in the role of the student at Columbia. . . . The greatest single phenomenon on the campus in the last 12 months has been the shift to radicalism, the development of the feeling that the usual, slow-moving methods of change are inadequate, and the growing attraction of more forceful action."

But for all the success of student power at Columbia, the administration did nothing to give permanency to the student voice, or to foster reforms in general. The clearest clue to the administration's disinclination to consider reform was President Grayson Kirk's refusal to implement, or even release, the Student Life Report submitted to him in August 1967.

This report was the result of two years of study by five administrators, five faculty members, and five students, all appointed by the president after the first student demonstration in May 1965. Four of the five student members issued a minority report rejecting the majority opinion as "too little and too late." But even the implementation of the majority's recommendations might have been sufficient to prevent the student revolt in April 1968.

The majority recommended that demonstrations inside buildings be allowed as long as they did not disrupt the normal functioning of the university. They proposed the establishment of judicial bodies, composed of students, faculty, and administrators, to impose and review discipline. They also recommended formation of student advisory committees on academic affairs in all departments and schools, and a university tripartite committee on student interests to advise the president.

The four students writing the minority report stated (with what now appears as unusual foresight) :

"We believe a tripartite committee on administrative policy should instead be created to decide important matters of non-academic policy, subject to the veto of the president or trustees. It would not make most policy or operating decisions within the university. That is quite properly the responsibility of the administrator. But it should deal with major questions which are of concern to all the elements of the university community. Such recent decisions as whether to involve Columbia in the business of promoting cigarette filters, whether to continue tuition deferment, and where or whether to build a gymnasium and how to allocate its facilities, serve as examples of the scope of the committee. Such matters as the physical expansion of the university, the university's relations with governments, and major policies of student conduct vis-a-vis the rest of the university community would be in the purview of the tripartite committee and its decisions would be policy unless vetoed by the president or trustees."

In September 1967, disregarding this Student Life Report, President Kirk banned all indoor demonstrations. Vice-President David Truman explained, "The administration will not tolerate efforts to make the university an instrument of opposition to the established order." Yet, in order to avoid a free-speech controversy, the administrators later interpreted the rule liberally (and often arbitrarily). They considered two indoor demonstrations early in the year as only "near demonstrations," and the participants were not punished. It was only in early April 1968 that the administration began to enforce the rule. At the same time, the president declined to follow either his own precedent of the year before, or the recommendations of the Student Life majority, by refusing to appoint a tripartite judicial body to try students accused of breaking the rule against indoor demonstrations.

This new ban—following the administration's concessions in 1967 and in the absence of effective channels for student grievances—helped discredit the administration's authority and helped legitimate direct-action tactics in the eyes of the students. Meanwhile, students for a Democratic Society and other radical groups had formed coalitions with moderate student groups. This was possible because, from March 1967 until Mark Rudd became president in March 1968, S.D.S. was run by moderates, who temporarily rejected direct-action techniques in favor of "research" to expose the administration and "education" to gain the allegiance of moderate students. The student radicals, therefore, had a broad base to mobilize for a student revolt.

In brief, the escalation of confrontation between students and administration from April to June 1968 consisted of:

■ a student sit-in at Hamilton Hall, the classroom and administration building of Columbia College, and the detention of a dean for 24 hours;

■ the occupation and barricading of five university buildings for five days by about 800 students;

■ the administration's calling of 1000 policemen to re-

move the demonstrators from the buildings, which resulted in the arrest of about 700 students and the injuring of 150 students and faculty;
- a massive strike by 5000 active students;
- the administration's "lock-out" to counter the strike —its canceling of formal classes and exams for the remainder of the school year;
- the start of disciplinary action against the student activists, which led to a second student sit-in at Hamilton Hall;
- the arrest of about 200 more students and the injuring of another 68 in a second police action;
- student violence during this second police action;
- the university's suspending of about 75 students.

The occupation of the five buildings and the subsequent student strike mobilized wide student support. Many of the official student leaders supported all of the demands of the occupation forces and even were leaders in the strike. While initially opposed to the barricading of buildings, these moderates saw the confrontation as an opportunity to win the student voice they had so long and fruitlessly sought. As they said later, two days at the barricades would probably accomplish more than years of work through legitimate channels. The moderates' prior use of direct-action techniques also conditioned them to accept more radical tactics.

Throughout the revolt there was solidarity between radical and moderate activists, despite disagreements and tensions. Moderates worked with the radical leaders of the Steering Committee that coordinated the occupation of four of the buildings (the black demonstrators maintained their separate leadership); this coalition continued in the Strike Steering Committee.

This solidarity encouraged the moderates to accept the occupation, the demand for amnesty, and the strike.

Later on, the radicals also accepted some of the moderates' stands on tactics and issues—the organization of the Strike Committee along representative lines, and an increased emphasis on the internal restructuring of the university. One reason for the trust between moderates and radicals was their interaction and coalition in former years; but more important was their common alienation from the administration and isolation from the faculty.

As the confrontation escalated, many students previously unaffiliated and politically inactive suddenly became involved, either in support of or in opposition to the sit-in. The strike that followed the police intervention generated more organization and solidarity among students, in the form of "liberated" classes and strike constituencies. In addition, ad-hoc student groups arose to proclaim grievances and make demands for change.

The specific events that propelled increasing numbers of students into confrontation with the administration can now be traced more closely.

In late March of 1968, S.D.S. sponsored a march to President Kirk's office to present a petition signed by 1700 students requesting the university's separation from the Institute of Defense Analyses. The president's response was to put six leaders of S.D.S. on probation for violating his ban on indoor demonstrations. The six students thereupon requested an open hearing before a tripartite judicial board, and were refused. On April 23, S.D.S. held a noon rally to organize a peaceful march into Low Library, the administration building, to present President Kirk with a demand for open

hearings for the six students. This march, like the previous one, would deliberately defy the ban on indoor
demonstrations. The April rally also repeated demands
for the university to cut all ties with I.D.A. and to stop
building a gym. Thus, this student movement simultaneously criticized the internal procedures of the university and its public policies.

When the demonstrators reached Low Library, they
found the door locked. In much confusion, between
200 and 300 students decided to march to the gym
site a few blocks away. After trying to rip down a
wire fence and being confronted by police, they returned to campus and voted to sit-in at Hamilton Hall.
That night the black students decided to occupy the
building by themselves, and asked the whites to leave.
Humiliated, white radicals decided spontaneously to
break into and occupy the president's office. During the
next two days, three additional buildings were occupied. The most militant acts—the detention of the
college dean for 24 hours, the occupation of the president's office, and the inspection of his files—alienated
many students. On the other hand, moderate students
were mobilized by the reorganization of Hamilton Hall
under black students and by the occupation of Avery
Hall by architecture students and of Fayerweather Hall
by graduate social-science students.

After the Student Afro-American Society took over
Hamilton Hall it erected barricades at the doors, an
act that was to become symbolic of all the "liberated"
buildings. This act was probably inspired by the Harlem radicals in the building who were not students.
But during the next two days, the course of events
inside Hamilton Hall was moderated. The black students became highly organized; they evicted the non-

students and allowed outsiders (like Rap Brown and Stokely Carmichael) to visit only for a short time; they released the dean; they cleaned the building and maintained it in good condition; they were open to visits and suggestions from professors, city officials, and Negro leaders; and they held numerous negotiations.

The graduate students took over Avery and Fayerweather somewhat haphazardly, but soon became organized. The architecture students had not been political in the past, but recently they had become resentful over university policies toward the community. Earlier in the year, the students and faculty of the School of Architecture had petitioned the administration to reconsider building the gym. Similarly, many of the graduate students in social science had never taken political action before, at least at Columbia, but had become more and more critical of the university's public policies.

Many students soon joined in the occupation of Avery and Fayerweather, and others visited the buildings (through the windows) to discuss the issues and give their support. Most of these students were not radicals and could not have seen themselves doing such a thing two days earlier. These occupations generated feelings of moral exhilaration and solidarity; the buildings were transformed into "communes" where the students engaged in lengthy political discussions.

Student support of the demonstrations was not limited to those willing to occupy buildings: The *Columbia Spectator* endorsed all the demands of the occupation —the end of university ties with I.D.A., no construction of a gym, the ending of probation for the six students, amnesty for all demonstrators in the occupation, and open hearings for all future disciplinary proceedings. A referendum held by undergraduate honor societies during the occupation, in which 5500 students voted, showed large majorities supporting the goals of the demonstrators, though not their tactics. Ten student leaders, including the president and vice-president of the university student government, came out in support of all the demonstration's demands, including amnesty. They also urged major university reform—including the establishment of faculty-student legislative and judicial bodies. Up to 800 students held vigils to support the rebels. (About 250 students opposed to the sit-ins tried to prevent students and food from reaching the demonstrators holding the president's office.)

After the police action, according to the Barton survey 42 percent of all students (and probably a much larger percentage of the undergraduates) supported a general boycott of all classes. A strike steering committee was formed of about 70 delegates, each representing 70 constitutents. Thus, almost 5000 students were actively organized, and many others boycotted classes. The Strike Committee supported all the original demands of the occupation and went on to demand a restructuring of the university.

The massive and militant student demonstrations immobilized the administration at first, but then were countered by the use of massive police force. The confrontation jarred part of the faculty into a belated, and ultimately unsuccessful, attempt to intervene between the students and the administration.

The great confrontation at Columbia did not lead to a successful negotiation between the students and the administration. In fact, bargaining never really began, for the administration and students could never agree on a basis for negotiation. Indeed, the administration did not seriously seek to negotiate. On the second day of the occupation, the administrators did present a proposal to the black students in Hamilton Hall, but when this was rejected they did not try again. The administration never presented a proposal for negotiating to the white students in the other four buildings. (According to the Barton survey, 50 percent of the faculty and 58 percent of the students thought the administration negotiated too little.)

It was ultimately the organizational weaknesses of Columbia that prevented any effective negotiations.

■ The administration, because of its isolation and lack of supporting structures, became fixated upon upholding its own authority. To negotiate would have accorded some legitimacy to students' grievances, and the administration found this too threatening.

■ The faculty, because of its weak organization and lack of experience in university government, could not counter the administration-student polarization.

The administration made every effort to discredit the demonstrators, but this served only to confirm the views of the most radical students and to strengthen their leadership.

Here were the students sitting in a few "liberated" buildings, with no weapons and with flimsy barricades of furniture, citing slogans of Che Guevara and Mao. But then the administration said that they *were* revolutionaries—"an unscrupulous bunch of revolutionaries out to destroy the university." The students said they would shut down the university; the administration did it for them. Four buildings and a president's office do not constitute a university, but the administration never tried to reschedule classes or to keep the university operating. A radical black leader kept saying that Harlem was marching up to Columbia to burn it down. Immediately the administration closed down the university and then sealed it off. It soon became a standing joke to ask, "When is the community coming?," for not more than 80 to 100 people from Harlem ever showed up.

Here were 800 student demonstrators, supported by all the moderate and legitimate student leaders. But the administration saw only a small minority of radical students organized by outside agitators. Even when Vice-President Truman admitted that there was increasing student support of amnesty, he said it was only because the "students don't understand what the fundamental issue is and they want to get on back to work."

Some of the radicals used vulgar language and obscenities in attacking the administration. Vice-President Truman in turn charged the activists with a "total lack of morality." Personal attacks upon President Kirk were countered with personal attacks upon the radical student leaders. Thus, Vice-President Truman said of Mark Rudd: "He is totally unscrupulous and morally very dangerous. He is an extremely capable, ruthless, cold-blooded guy. He's a combination of a revolutionary and an adolescent having a temper tantrum. . . . It makes me uncomfortable to sit in the same room with him."

The radicals pictured Columbia University, its president and its trustees, as part of the American power structure. And the administrators acted so as to seemingly confirm their dependence upon external groups rather than upon students and faculty. During the crisis, the administrators were isolated from all the students and most of the faculty. They remained cloistered in Low Library, consulting almost exclusively with trustees, Mayor Lindsay, and other outside advisers. The president and vice-president never talked directly and publicly to the demonstrators or to other students. Only once did they meet personally (but secretly) with several of the student leaders.

This approach to the students helped solidify their distrust of the administration and their determination to resist its authority. The issue of amnesty became the focus of distrust between students and administrators. From the first day of the occupation, the students demanded amnesty as a prerequisite to negotiation on the other issues. From the first, the administration refused to consider amnesty.

The student demonstrators sought amnesty as a confirmation of their position. In the words of the Strike Committee:

"Our demand for amnesty implies a specific political point. Our actions are legitimate; it is the laws, and the administration's policies which the laws have been designed to protect, that are illegitimate. It is therefore ridiculous to talk about punishment for students. No one suggests punishment for the administration, who in fact must assume the guilt for the present situation. To consider discipline against the students is thus a political position."

In addition, the activists did not trust the administration to radically change its policies, and therefore they sought to protect the students from even a relatively light punishment, like probation. (A student "on probation" could be suspended for slight infractions during future demonstrations.)

Conversely, the administration saw the granting of any form of amnesty as a capitulation that would undermine its authority. Vice-President Truman said later: "We couldn't give on the amnesty thing at all. Not only would we be destroying the whole position of this university, with that one we'd have been destroying every other university in the country." (It seems that the presidents of Stanford, Northwestern, and France were not listening, for during subsequent weeks they granted amnesty to *their* student rebels.) Hence, during the first days of the occupation the administration told the radical leaders, with great emotion and vehemence, that they would be expelled.

Not only did the administrators refuse amnesty for students, but they also rejected a compromise designed by an ad-hoc faculty group. This faculty group proposed light and equal punishments for all demonstrators, to be imposed by new forms of due process. (The Barton survey found that 78 percent of the students and 69 percent of the faculty believed that all judicial decisions on student discipline should be made in open hearings by a committee of students and faculty.) But the administration twice refused this compromise, and instead resorted to police force.

Twelve hours before using the police the first time in April, President Kirk had accepted the "spirit" of the faculty proposal, but had rejected most of its substance. Among other things, he refused to give up his authority to make the final decision on student discipline; and he refused to agree beforehand to uniform penalties for all the demonstrators. When the students also refused to accept the ad-hoc faculty's compromise, the administration cited the "intransigence" of the demonstrators as justifying their own resort to police force.

Again in May, the president refused to give final

authority on discipline to the then-operating Joint Committee on Discipline. After a huge outcry from the faculty, and pressure behind the scenes from both faculty and trustees, he retreated somewhat, but still refused to accept any specific long-range limitations on his authority. The Joint Committee on Discipline also recommended that the university not undertake disciplinary action while criminal charges against certain students were pending in the courts. But one week later the administration called four student leaders to the dean's office for a closed hearing. Most student leaders interpreted these summonses as an attempt to reestablish the former disciplinary procedures behind a thin facade of reform. The four students, therefore, did not appear (both to protect their legal rights in court and to protest the administrators' action), but sent their parents and lawyers instead. This was unacceptable to the administrators, who immediately suspended the four students.

These suspensions seemed deliberately provocative to the demonstrators, and were countered by a second student sit-in. This time the administration announced that it would call the police that same evening, and that anyone arrested would be immediately suspended. Again, the administration, in threatening automatic suspensions, made no reference to the new disciplinary committee or to new judicial procedures. Thus, as the *Columbia Spectator* stated on May 22: "The administration and the strikers yesterday engaged in a test of strength where there was no buffer of faculty intermediaries and no chance of a compromise settlement. Both groups were committed to holding the line against what they regarded as the illegitimate opposition of the other."

There is some evidence that both the administration and the radical student leaders *wanted* the use of the police, at least the first time. The activists believed that the use of the police to clear the buildings would radicalize the campus, and bring many more students and faculty to their side. This did happen after the first police action. (According to the Barton survey, faculty support for the sit-ins increased by 17 percent and student support by 19 percent.) The administration, on the other hand, believed that the police were needed to restore its authority. Vice-President Truman said that "there were only two alternatives: either to give in or to bring in the police."

The result of the police intervention was to create an atmosphere of violence, contempt, and hatred. It was during the second police action that students for the first time became violent—throwing bricks at the police, smashing windows, and perhaps starting fires in several buildings. Apolitical, nonviolent students were enraged at seeing policemen beat their friends, many of whom were only spectators. Apolitical, nonviolent professors were enraged by the burning of a professor's research papers and by fires set in university buildings. After both police actions, the mood on campus was one of outrage.

Yet the administration maintained its confrontation mentality and became even more committed to a strategy of force and repression. Vice-President Truman commented to the press in May that the most important lesson he had learned from the Columbia crisis was to call the police immediately to oust student demonstrators. In June, President Kirk suspended 75 students for their part in the second sit-in. At the same time, the president continued to maintain that there was nothing fundamentally wrong with the university, and that no positive changes were possible in a crisis atmosphere. In response, the student activists—even the moderates—vowed to continue mass action against the university.

The long history of disorganization and withdrawal of the Columbia faculty members prevented them, at first, from taking any stand on the student demonstration. No faculty faction was organized to directly support the students. Nor was there any effectively organized support for the administration. The one attempt by the administration to organize faculty support was to call an unprecedented meeting of the Joint Faculties on Morningside Heights. Two meetings were convened—one right before the first police action and one right after. In both cases, the assembly passed mild, noncommittal statements, which neither condemned nor supported the administration. The meetings were presided over by the president and vice-president, thereby attesting to the faculty's lack of an independent role in university government. Because this body had no independence, no experience, and no leaders, it was unable to seek a solution to the confrontation.

During the first part of the crisis, only an ad-hoc faculty group was active. The original organizers of this group included 34 tenured professors, 38 assistant professors, and 84 teachers below that rank. Its membership grew to an active core of about 200. Members of the ad-hoc faculty had many different positions and views on the crisis, but they tended to be more sympathetic to the students than were other faculty members. Many (especially those from Columbia College) had close personal relations with their students, including some of the demonstrators, and some in the past had been among the few faculty activists on university issues. The younger teachers, especially, to a great degree shared the ideals, political frustrations, and disaffection from the university that had propelled the students into the buildings. (Barton's survey of 769 faculty members showed that tenured faculty members were most conservative on all issues, and instructors most favorable to the demonstrations. For example, 12 percent of full professors thought the sit-ins were justified, 38 percent of assistant professors, and 48 percent of lecturers and instructors.) The one purpose that did unite the ad-hoc faculty was a strong stand against the use of the police to resolve the dispute. For five days, members sought a basis for negotiation in order to prevent police action.

From its beginning, the ad-hoc faculty recognized the fierce antagonism between the administration and the demonstrators. And because it had so little active support from the senior faculty and no constitutional status, the ad-hoc group itself was propelled into the politics of confrontation in attempting to persuade the antagonists to accept its efforts at compromise. Its first statement, which shocked many faculty members, made two threats to the administration:

(1) "Should the students be willing to evacuate the buildings on the basis of our proposals, we will not meet classes until the crisis is resolved along these lines."

(2) "Until the crisis is settled, we will stand before the occupied buildings to prevent forcible entry by police or others."

The motive behind these threats was to win credibility from the students and administration, without taking a stand on amnesty. It worked—for a while.

On the third day of the confrontation, Vice-President Truman came to the ad-hoc faculty's meeting to announce that the president had called the police. The faculty present arose in indignation, with shouts of "Shame!" A few of the leaders rushed to the president's office; the rest went and stood in front of the occupied buildings. After several faculty members were physically attacked by a small contingent of policemen seeking entry to the administration building, the president ordered the police to withdraw. He thus granted the ad-hoc faculty a little more time to seek a negotiated settlement.

The ad-hoc faculty, in trying to find a basis for negotiation between the administration and student demonstrators, sought to apply pressure on both sides without itself taking a clear stand on the issues. While strongly disagreeing with the administration's position (and with some of the student actions), the leaders of the ad-hoc faculty never clearly broke with the administration. Nor did they try to organize the senior faculty members and win their active support for the group's proposals. In the Joint Faculties meeting called by the administration, the ad-hoc faculty declined to ask for a vote on its proposal for arbitration. Even though the ad-hoc faculty's leaders believed they could have won a small majority, they did not want to split the faculty, or risk the possibility of being rebuffed by the trustees.

On only one occasion—the day before the first police action—did the ad-hoc faculty try to bolster its position by mobilizing mass support. On that day it obtained 800 faculty and 3000 student signatures, and the support of some city and state political leaders. But these supporters were not an organized constituency that could be mobilized for action. Thus, when both students and administration refused to accept its compromise settlement, the ad-hoc faculty had no alternative plan to check the polarization between administration and students or to block the police action. Even at the zero hour, when both the president and the students had rejected their proposal and they knew that police intervention was imminent, the ad-hoc faculty members could only frantically vote to call on either Governor Rockefeller or Mayor Lindsay to arbitrate the dispute.

It was this reluctance of the faculty to adopt a clear position, rather than trying to find a compromise, that most alienated the student protestors. This was especially true in view of the fact that the faculty institutions were so weak and faculty members had been so inactive in the past. The students did not believe that the ad-hoc faculty could really influence the administration without its taking a stronger stand. Right before the first police intervention, some of the more moderate students occupying Avery and Fayerweather hinted that they were ready to talk about alternatives to complete amnesty, as suggested by the ad-hoc faculty's proposals. But then they decided that they had to stay with the amnesty demand because the ad-hoc faculty did not seem to them to be sufficiently dependable.

The morning after the first police action, the ad-hoc faculty group dissolved in chaos. It was completely alienated by the administration's resort to force. (Many of these faculty members had witnessed the police action and some were injured by the police.) But the group was unable to agree on a common strategy towards the administration. Successive faculty groups also failed to change the administration's stand on discipline and its reliance upon the use of force, nor did they gain the trust and support of the students.

The faculty thus failed to check the escalating polarization and confrontation between students and administration. This failure shocked the faculty into a recognition of the need for fundamental institutional reform.

Even before the first police action, some students and faculty members recognized that one result of the conflict would have to be major changes in the university. After the police action, the predominant issue became the restructuring of the university. But student and faculty reformers held different conceptions of how this restructuring would occur and of the ends to be achieved. (The Barton survey found a relatively small difference in answers given by students and faculty on the issues of the crisis, except on items dealing with the relative power of students and faculty in a restructured university. Here the differences were greater than 20 percent.)

Th student activists believed that real change in the university could be obtained and institutionalized only if the crisis continued. Faculty reformers argued that important institutional restructuring could occur only slowly, after careful study in a less stressful atmosphere. The latter envisioned *reform* of the university from above, through the work of a few appointed *committees*. The students desired a *change* from below, through the participation of *constituencies*. Faculty members viewed both the process and results of university reform in *professional* terms; that is, decisions should be made by those with the most relevant expertise. To improve Columbia's educational quality and institutional effectiveness, what was needed, they believed, was a new *rational-legal* organization (more and better committees and courts, and a more progressive administration). The students, on the other hand, wanted the university to divorce itself from existing centers of power and to contribute to the solution of major social and human problems. The students recognized that the professional competence of professors and even administrators would prevail on many technical and academic issues, but they insisted that students as well as faculty must *participate* in setting the university's general public and educational policies.

One incident during the faculty's early efforts at reform illustrates the preference of faculty leaders for change from above by committee, rather than by participatory organization from below—for discussion in private by experts, rather than open deliberation and debate.

In the general outrage after the first police action, the ad-hoc faculty group held an extraordinary meeting. Its steering committee introduced a strong resolution to its members (and to many other faculty members present) that expressed no confidence in the administration and supported the student strike. The resolution obviously would have passed, but during the debate the chairman withdrew the resolution and, along with the steering committee, left the meeting. What happened was that these faculty members began to fear that their resolution was too radical and that it might further polarize the faculty and university community. Later that same day, the leaders of the ad-hoc faculty supported a resolution in the Joint Faculties meeting calling for the establishment of an executive committee of the faculty to propose university reforms. Half of the ad-hoc faculty's leaders were appointed to this committee of 12, and the ad-hoc faculty group was thus dissolved.

The new Executive Committee of the Faculty (in contrast to the ad-hoc faculty group) had ready access to the trustees and enjoyed the confidence of the administration, but it had neither a constituency nor any clear mandate. The ad-hoc faculty had begun, at least, to build a participating constituency. Although the Executive Committee could call meetings of the Joint Faculties, it never did. Its work was done behind closed doors, and as a group it became invisible to most of the campus. During the second police action, and on the arguments over discipline, it publicly supported the administration, and worked only secretly to pressure the president and vice-president to adopt a more conciliatory stand. Such procedures did not gain it the confidence and support of the students.

Moreover, in its first month of work (to the end of the academic year), the Executive Committee failed to formulate any principles for restructuring the university that could have been publicly debated, but simply organized a series of study groups for the summer. Students and faculty were asked to join the paid staff of these committees, but no campaign was undertaken to actively recruit such members. In any case, most concerned students viewed such committees as an inadequate response to the crisis. Even the moderate students most committed to restructuring the university feared being coopted through their participation in such efforts. Another new faculty group, the Independent Faculty, formed out of the remaining 15 leaders of the ad-hoc faculty, also failed to organize a real constituency.

The student organizations pressing for reform were

much different. Representation on the Steering Committee to lead the strike was based upon constituencies. Any group of 70 students could elect a member to the Strike Steering Committee. Subsequently, the Steering Committee split, about half of its members withdrawing to form their own organization, Students for a Restructured University. This new organization wanted to give primary emphasis to the internal reform of the university; the Strike Committee was more concerned with political conflicts of the larger society, and with the relationship of the university to these political issues. Both groups continued to support the original demands of the sit-ins, and to vigorously oppose the administration. Both continued to organize students. The two groups also united on special issues, and both remained suspicious of faculty organizations. In addition to these two student groups, caucuses arose in many school and graduate departments to press for educational and institutional reform. This proliferation of student groups backing the reform of the university was in sharp contrast to the lack of faculty participation.

At present, the faculty committees are in extremely weak positions vis-à-vis the administration and trustees. Within the Faculty Executive Committee, there is probably a powerful minority that supports the administration and wants only minimal change. Moreover, the Executive Committee does not have the support of most students. Even more troublesome is the extent of the faculty's division over whether students should take part in university decision-making. About half of the faculty are willing to grant students some decision-making power, according to Barton, but the others favor only regular consultation with them.

It thus seems evident that it is only through organizing constituencies that the faculty committed to reform at Columbia will be able to achieve real change in the university, or even to recreate its basic cohesion. Faculty reform leaders will have to assert organized pressure to gain ascendency and to make sure that new university committees, judicial bodies, and legislative organs are not just appointed from above, but receive general consent. Yet it is still questionable whether faculty leaders will arise and make the attempt. Columbia, therefore, faces more polarization, confrontation, and probably repression.

It was the great and increasing polarization between administrators, students, and faculty that prevented a solution to the Columbia student revolt. In this polarization the moderate positions were destroyed: Student moderates became radicalized, administration moderates became rigid and conservative, faculty moderates failed in attempts to mediate and became alienated from both sides. The weakness of the moderates was a result of the institutional weaknesses of Columbia— the archaic and isolated nature of administrative authority, the lack of effective faculty and student governments, and the attenuation of faculty-student relations. These institutional weaknesses led to a general lack of administrative and faculty responsiveness to student grievances and to the students' attempt to compel response by dramatic action.

A critical problem of Columbia, then, is to strengthen all components of the university in order to render them more responsive to one another. Even the administration requires strengthening—not, however, apart from students and faculty, but by new links to them. The forging of multiple institutional relations *within* the university can increase the interdependence of students, faculty, and administration, and simultaneously decrease dependence upon external forces (especially for the administration, but also for the faculty and even for the students).

Only then can the university fully develop its own capacities for intellectual and moral excellence, and independently determine its social responsibilities.

September 1968

The Crisis
At San Francisco State

JAMES MC EVOY/ABRAHAM MILLER

{

On Monday, December 2, of last year we traveled from the
placid setting of the Davis Campus of the University of
California to San Francisco State College, where student
strikers and the administration had been battling for control of the campus for more than a month. Our intention
in undertaking this trip was to interview students and faculty about the disorder and learn some of the reasons for
the intense level of conflict—which was occurring on a
campus marked, only a few years ago, by a generally
phlegmatic student body. Acting President S.I. Hayakawa's
hard-line policy toward the student demonstrators and the
strikers would also, we thought, allow us to evaluate the
success of authoritarian methods in dealing with dissident
students.

After talking with several dozen students and faculty
members, we decided that the situation was much more
complex than we had at first believed, that the press had
badly distorted what was happening on the campus, and

57

that—to this writing at least—the hard-line policy had served only to exacerbate the conflict and increase the number of policemen and demonstrators now contending for control of the campus.

We followed this first visit by a second, on December 4. December 3 had been a day of violence (more than 30 arrests were made), and we felt it would give us more insight into the situation if we could determine what effect the police action had had on the students and faculty. What follows is an analysis of both of our experiences at State and a discussion of the background and the implications of the conflict for higher education in the United States.

Late in 1967, there was a severe disruption of State's campus. Members of the Black Students Union (B.S.U.), enraged at what they thought were racist implications in an article in the *Daily Gator* (the school's paper), invaded the editorial offices and assaulted the editors. At the time of the *Gator* invasion, John Summerskill was president of State. Summerskill faced a situation in which left-liberal support for the B.S.U.'s actions was strong enough to mount a sizable demonstration in the group's favor. Marching to the administration building on Dec. 6, 1967, students and at least one faculty member (John Gerassi, author of *The Boys of Boise*) broke into the building; other buildings were also attacked. While the school's trustees (including Governor Ronald Reagan and Superintendent of Public Instruction Max Rafferty) were calling the police to restore order, Summerskill closed the campus.

By the end of the third week in February, Summerskill's authority was shaky at best. Faced with increasingly violent incidents on the campus and more and more right-wing pressure from the trustees, he chose a course that satisfied neither side. On February 22, 1968, he tendered his resignation, effective the following September. By the end of May, however, Chancellor Glen Dumke, Reagan, Rafferty, and the other conservative trustees were even more enraged by the continuing disorders. On May

24, Summerskill was fired: He had not taken a hard-enough line. His successor, Robert Smith, fared little better. Although the level of campus disruption had declined, Smith still faced a board of trustees, now openly led by Reagan, that was determined to clamp down on radicals. The clamp-down came when Reagan was informed that George Murray, the recently appointed Minister of Education of the Black Panthers, had been hired as an instructor in the English Department and had given a black-power speech, which advocated that minority students arm themselves for self-protection. On September 26, Dumke "requested" that Smith transfer Murray to a nonteaching job. Smith demurred. On October 31, Dumke ordered the suspension of Murray both as student and instructor. On November 1, Smith complied. Within a week, a strike was called by the B.S.U. and various radical white groups. And within two weeks, the campus had been closed on the orders of the new Acting President, Semanticist S.I. Hayakawa, who had replaced Smith on November 26. Smith found, as had his predecessor Summerskill, that the trustees simply would not let him make the decisions. They had ordered Murray suspended against Smith's wishes, and had insisted on keeping the campus open in the face of Smith's desire to close it.

On December 2, the morning we arrived on campus, we were greeted by a student representing the Committee for an Academic Environment, which was committed to keeping the campus open, despite the American Federation of Teachers (A.F.T.) strike. He was dispensing blue ribbons to be worn as armbands by students supporting the new president's decision to keep the campus open —with police force, if necessary. The student told us that he thought people had a right to strike, but that others, like himself, "had a right to learn." Students like himself, he went on, had no objection to most of the demands of the strikers (a series of 15 conditions put forward by the B.S.U., including the establishment of a black studies department and the reinstatement of George Murray) ; his only objection was to the tactics of the strikers. Most of the other students we talked with also supported these demands, but many—while angry about the strikers' tactics—believed that the strikers were justified in view of the unnecessarily authoritarian controls imposed on the administration, faculty, and students. The students saw Dumke, Reagan, and the trustees as unresponsive to their needs or desires, rigid and uncompromising. From these students we learned that the reports in the local press of classroom violence and intimidation had been much exaggerated. Typically, in the first stage of the strike, members of the Strike Committee would knock on the door of a classroom and request "five minutes" to present their position to the students. Usually, they were admitted after a vote of the class, and proceeded to give their side of the issues. This was, we found, the modal experience of those nonstriking students we talked with who had been in a class entered by the Strike Committee. But, an active member of the Committee told us, "We simply asked for five or ten minutes. Most of the time we were allowed to speak. A couple of times we went on longer, took up the whole period. Occasionally, though, fistfights did break out in classes. Later, the tactics were changed. After the convocation a general meeting to discuss the B.S.U. demands broke down. For the first time, it was the policy of all the groups to simply go into classes and try to dismiss the classes. Then, naturally, more fistfights occurred."

While some students liked Hayakawa and others did not, and while some approved of his actions and others did not, *almost all stated or implied that he lacked any real authority*. His decisions were not seen as binding; almost all of the students thought that his edicts originated with the trustees and Reagan, and were totally subject to their review. The consequence of this is that Hayakawa cannot bargain effectively. On the one hand, he is faced with a student body that knows his decisions are only pseudo-decisions, and therefore many of these students refuse to even discuss their demands with him. On the other hand, Reagan and the other trustees want "no negotiation" with the militants.

Most of the students we encountered also did not see Hayakawa as an effective executive. One said, "The trustees will use him as long as they can, and then get somebody else. It really doesn't matter." The crisis, most students felt, was not going to be resolved—at least from their side of the avenue. Most white students, generally supporting the demands of the B.S.U., believed that there would be no compromise, that the crisis would continue, that the police would remain on campus, and that Hayakawa had only shortened the fuse on an already explosive situation.

On Monday beginning at noon, an "illegal" rally (under Section III of the "Declaration of Emergency" issued by Hayakawa that morning) began on the speakers' platform —an area in the middle of the large quadrangle around which the campus buildings are spaced. About 500 people assembled at first, then gradually their number increased to at least 2,000, although only the first group was militant. The speeches of various black and white militants were highly emotional and slightly incoherent. Allusions to First Amendment freedoms were mixed together with the moral imperatives of the Nuremburg judgment. In their view, the strikers represented absolute good; the nonstrikers, the president, Reagan, Rafferty, the trustees, and the Establishment represented absolutely absolute evil.

By 1:30 p.m., the crowd of about 500 hard-core supporters had moved across the quad to the administration building, there to be addressed by B.S.U. members, including Murray and members of the Third World Liberation Front (T.W.L.F.). They screamed for an appearance by Hayakawa. This call unanswered, a move developed to occupy the building. At this point, Hayakawa summoned the San Francisco Police Department's Tactical Squad. As we watched from the roof of the administration building, the Tac Squad marched in formation, six abreast, and occupied the lobby of the building. The students retreated and went back to speechmaking. After about 20 minutes the Tac Squad withdrew. And within a few minutes, the militant portion of the crowd grew intensely hostile; shouting began again, and six or eight bricks, some previously hidden in lunch bags, were thrown at or through the windows of the building. The Tac Squad returned; the students and strikers (now numbering about 3,000 and 400 respectively) moved to a classroom building and began to disrupt classes by making noise outside—the police inside had prevented the crowd's entry. The Tac Squad then moved in front of the building. The strikers scattered, but returned to pelt the police with broken flower pots, rocks, and sod, then moved on to another building to repeat the performance. Within 15 minutes, about 250 more police were on the commons and by 3 P.M. the strikers had been dispersed. We did not observe a single instance of police violence.

This same series of events was repeated on Tuesday, except that this time the police *were* violent, chasing students into the cafeteria and beating some innocent bystanders.

We returned to State on Wednesday—partly to get more information and partly to assess the effects of the police violence the day before. Student after student told us he felt that the police were "only making things worse." In view of the growing crowds, the students were evidently correct. The police force had grown to nearly 1,000. The student strikers now numbered about 1,500.

On that day there was a rally, during which "members of the community" spoke for over an hour. Much of what was said—by blacks, Orientals, Mexicans, Filipinos, a state legislator, representatives from C.O.R.E. and the Urban League, and self-styled black moderates—would have sounded very familiar to those who have followed the recent school crisis in New York. "This is *our* school, and these are *our* kids, and we are not going to let Reagan or Hayakawa tell us how to run *our* school," said one nearly hysterical speaker. In her mind and in the minds of the hundreds who applauded her, the college must have become their personal property. Meanwhile, the Governor and the trustees tried to run *their* campus in their own way, presumably also acting as delegates for the outraged citizens, who, as taxpayers, felt that they were entitled to their say about how *their* campus was run.

Some portion of almost every daily television newscast in and around the Bay Area is devoted to the latest incidents at San Francisco State. The details of the almost daily encounters between police and students—from December 2 until the premature dismissal of classes for the holidays on December 13—made front-page news in almost every northern California daily. But while the public is saturated with detail, description, and moving pictures of confrontations, broken glass, and bloodied heads, little has been done to acquaint it with the full dimensions of the issues.

The reluctance of the media to provide any analysis of the situation is not the result of a noble attempt to refrain from taking sides. Acting President Hayakawa has been interviewed repeatedly on television, while spokesmen for the dissidents have not been. In and around the Bay Area, people hold strong opinions about the events at San Francisco State in spite of an appalling degree of ignorance. Those people we talked with often prefaced their comments with, "Well, the situation is very complex but. . . ." When questioned *about* the complexity of the situation, these people apparently for the first time realized just how little they knew about what was taking place at San Francisco State and—more important—*why* it was taking place.

The crisis, as noted, was caused by the suspension of George Murray. President Smith, fully aware that Murray's suspension without a hearing would bring black militants and white liberals together in opposition to the administration, attempted to forestall any action against Murray until the normal academic procedural mechanisms could be brought into play. Chancellor Dumke and the trustees decided to intervene because they were hardly prepared to indulge Murray with legal procedures.

Murray has said that he himself is not an issue.

Even the majority of students we interviewed from the Committee for an Academic Environment (C.A.E.), the committee supporting the get-tough policies of President Hayakawa, felt that the trustees had brought the crisis upon themselves by refusing to consider student demands that had been brought repeatedly to their attention. The C.A.E. also felt that no set of demands was important enough to bring about the closing of the school, and here lay its members' fundamental difference with the strikers.

Hayakawa himself gave public notice on several occasions that he thought the demands were justified and acceded to most of them, including the formation of a black-studies program and the appointment of Professor Nathan Hare as its head, with power equal to that of any other department chairman. Although there was no unanimity in accepting the truth of Hayakawa's public statements, one of the black faculty members informed us that many of the blacks believed in Hayakawa's sincerity but felt that his sentiments were worthless—because the role he had been called upon to play was simply one of a puppet. With Reagan and Rafferty pulling the strings, the blacks felt there was little appreciable value in the public pronouncements of the "Governor's marionette."

Our respondents repeatedly called for the preservation of accepted procedures of due process, the right of political dissent and academic freedom, the right of the students to have a voice in their education, and the exclusion of the chancellor and the trustees from affairs that were perceived as falling under the jurisdiction of the campus administration. Students and faculty, of almost all shades of opinion, saw these issues as the underlying causes of the crisis. But in contrast to the whites, black students tended to ignore the "larger issues," and to emphasize the demands being made by the B.S.U. and the Third World Liberation Front. The blacks spoke of very pragmatic and visible goals the attainment of which required not rhetoric but results.

When we questioned white students and faculty about specific illustrations of their more general concerns, we found that we were opening a floodgate of long-standing grievances. Among them: the resignation last winter of President John Summerskill rather than submit to the trustees' demand that the police be brought on campus to squelch a disturbance; the intervention of Chancellor Dumke in forcing Smith to suspend George Murray; the subsequent resignation of Smith in face of the get-tough policy of the trustees, the dismissal of Professors John R. Martinez and John Gerassi for their political views; the denial of tenure to Professor William Stanton for his role in the strike, and to Professor Patrick Gleeson for no apparent reason other than his initial responsibility in hiring Murray; and the lack of action on programs that a majority of students and faculty felt should have been implemented, including the trustees rejection of the design (by Moshe Safdie, designer of Habitat, Montreal Expo '68) of the proposed student union, though the building will be completely paid for and operated by students.

Hayakawa, Dumke, and Reagan, in a special telecast dealing with the problems at State, charged that the "silent majority" of students and faculty do not support the strikers and want to have the college return to normality. But if the majority stands against the strikers, why does it stand so silently? In a December 17 letter to the *San Francisco Chronicle,* Frederic W. Terrien, a professor of sociology at State, raised this very issue: "What keeps the majority silent is this very disenchantment [because of the Reagan Administration's lack of support for the state-college system] together with the sharp awareness that some of the militants' demands should long since have been college policy." Terrien went on to say that even if Hayakawa, whom Terrien supports, succeeds in keeping the college open, "the chancellor, most of the trustees, and the Governor will back off and sell him short on what is really required for change and growth. Save for the company of [San Francisco] Mayor Alioto and a few trustees, Dr. Hayakawa stands alone."

One of our major concerns was how students and faculty would react not only to the appointment of Hayakawa but to the manner in which he was appointed. Prior to the opening of school after the Thanksgiving recess, Professor Leo G. McClatchy, head of the Academic Senate, disclosed in a televised interview his displeasure with the hurried procedure used to appoint Hayakawa. To many, it was another case of the trustees disregarding the autonomy of the institution and the opinions of its faculty. What McClatchy did not point out in his interview was that the five most probable candidates for Robert Smith's position had agreed among themselves that no one would accept the office without prior consultation with the other four men. Apparently, this collaboration could have been used to gain some concessions from the trustees. Hayakawa and McClatchy were among the five; when appointed, Hayakawa did not consult with the other members.

We found, surprisingly, that the students and faculty were generally unconcerned with the nature of Hayakawa's appointment. As they explained, the manner of making an appointment to an office that is already illegitimate is completely irrelevant. When the students rallied outside of Hayakawa's office the Monday afternoon prior to the outbreak of violence, their rallying cry was, "We want the puppet, we want the puppet."

If nothing else, it is clear that the educational leaders, by responding like a 19th century vigilante committee to the problems of both the University of California system and the state-college system, have won a few battles. They have succeeded in removing a few radicals from the campus, in forcing the resignation of unsubmissive presidents (including Clark Kerr), in restricting the academic role of

Eldridge Cleaver on the Berkeley campus and in rescinding credit for the sociology course he was giving. The price they paid for these and similar victories was higher than they have imagined or yet realized. In winning the battles, they have in effect lost the war.

The enforcement of decisions of authority is a police function. And when authority is viewed as illegitimate, the police are viewed as armed mercenaries. From the perspective of the dissidents, the police in the final analysis are free men. As free men they are presumed by the students to have a right to choose whether they will implement the whims of a capricious and illegitimate authority—or refuse.

In defiance of Hayakawa's suspension of civil liberties, as mentioned, black militants and their white supporters held a rally on the commons. Shortly after the rally began, the head of the campus police, in plain clothes, and surrounded by three uniformed members of the Tac Squad, approached the speakers' platform to inform the strikers that they were in defiance of the emergency order. The sight of the police on campus enraged the crowd. One attractive, neatly dressed girl standing next to us distorted her face in anger, raised her hand in a clenched fist, and shouted, "Up against the wall, you mother-fucking bastards!" Similar and sometimes more creative obscenities thundered from the crowd. A chant developed, "Get their guns, get their guns." The police withdrew.

There is no doubt in our minds that one of the results of the "police riot" in Chicago during the Democratic convention—Daley's Folly—is that it has hampered the effective use of the police against students for generations to come. Everywhere today, including State, the reaction of students to the police is completely emotional.

During the crisis at State, it is to Hayakawa's credit that he used the Tac Squad judiciously: bringing it in and having it depart as soon as some temporary order was restored. This limited use of the police frustrated the militants, and in their anger at being ignored, they escalated the use of force to compel Hayakawa to call in the police in large numbers and to keep them on campus. The militant blacks called for action, and a few people in the crowd threw rocks at the administration building. Then the police appeared on the scene to disperse the crowd. It was obvious that one of the reasons for the militant's desire to bring the cops on campus was to capitalize on the students' blind hatred of the police.

With the police lines protecting the administration building, the dissident students moved to the business school, an object of special animosity to the strikers because the business-school students and faculty were overwhelmingly against the strike. But the dissidents were unable to disrupt the classes—the building was protected by a contingent of police. And despite rather strong provocation, the police stood firm: absorbing punishment rather than charging the students and causing even greater hostility. Later, the continued assaults on the police, the disruptions of classes, and attacks on property led to the clearing of the campus.

Despite the restraint of the police Monday afternoon, students responded by seeing what they thought they should see rather than what actually occurred. Feigning ignorance of what had gone on, we asked respondents on the scene, "What happened?" Dissident students told us that the police provoked the violence by charging the crowd. The fact that Hayakawa held the police off campus and called them only after the windows in the administration building were broken was not mentioned, nor was the fact that at that point the police had not laid a hand on one student although they had been pelted with everything from a 24-inch-long pipe to broken flower pots.

A group of girls who had been in a modern-dance class, completely ignorant of the immediately preceding events, came rushing out shouting, "Get those mother-fucking pigs off campus!" One of the girls volunteered to us that the "fucking pigs" caused all the violence—although she had just emerged from a basement gymnasium that provided no view of the Commons.

We are at a loss to explain the restraint of the police on Monday and their violence against innocent bystanders on Tuesday—for with regard to Tuesday, the accusations against the police came from both strikers and nonstrikers alike. News films added even more credibility to these reports. Many of the students who had been on the fringe of the movement swelled into the ranks of the strikers after Tuesday's violence. One girl said that up until Tuesday her main concern had been getting back into class, but after witnessing the beating of a Students for a Democratic Society (S.D.S.) co-chairman by the police, she felt she had to side with the strikers.

We found it interesting that the brutality of the police increased some students' support for the strikers, but the brutality of the strikers toward the police did not diminish any students' support for the strikers. To the students, violence against the police is tolerable. Consequently, the administration was caught in the position of either turning the buildings over to the students, or calling in the police and swelling the strikers' ranks.

The presence of the police, in addition, was clearly used by the strikers as a way of playing on the hostility of the students toward the police and thus to increase support for the strikers. The police, an ostensible tool of authority, have been manipulated into a tool of the forces opposing authority.

We repeatedly asked white students and faculty that if the larger issues were of major concern, why did they not involve themselves more actively in the leadership of the movement? White student activists pointed out that the authorities (usually white) are most noticeably repressive against blacks, and as soon as the reactionaries move against the blacks, usually the white liberals move in and take over. Thus, the whites forget the black needs. And this misguided continuation of the plantation mentality, the white student activists told us, has got to stop. "We support the blacks," one white militant said, "despite the fact that we disagree with some of their demands and some of their tactics. What is really important is for the black students to create their own sense of identity. By supporting them and not imposing ourselves into the leadership positions, we foster the creation of that identity, the fulfillment of their immediate needs, and our own concerns with the larger issues at stake."

Charles Hamilton, the noted black political scientist, has said that white student movements differ from black student movements in that the former are directed at abstract and symbolic goals while the latter are directed toward realistic goals. To some extent, our own observations confirm those of Hamilton. The immediate tangible demands of the blacks were in themselves of little interest to the white militants. For the blacks, the issues were, to a large extent, out on the table.

No observer could fail to recognize that San Francisco State was a testing ground for both sides to determine the necessary costs of victory. The get-tough policy of Hayakawa could find its roots in a dozen pronouncements by Reagan and Rafferty. Similarly, the actions of the hard-core militants had firm foundation in the rhetoric of Eldridge Cleaver and George Murray. On a picturesque campus in San Francisco on Dec. 2, 1968 the fascism of the left and the fascism of the right were to begin the test of each other's mettle. Predictions of victory are premature, but there is little doubt that higher education in California will be the first casualty of the encounter.

There may have been some ironic delight in the trustees' appointment of Hayakawa. Black militants would now have to confront a yellow man with the taunt of "white racist."

Hayakawa, in addition to the color of his skin and his impeccable academic credentials, had served as a newspaper-man for *Chicago's Defender,* a Negro newspaper. He himself took the position that the militants did not speak for the Negro community or for other minority groups. They were a noisy rabble, hell-bent on destruction. Decent black men like decent white men had no use for them.

The militants were not to be so readily destroyed, for it was easy for them to characterize Hayakawa as a "Tom," a "Tojo Tom," a puppet of the administration. The strongest blow at Hayakawa as a spokesman for the silent majority of whites and ethnics, too, came from a "representative" of the Japanese community, who attempted to make it clear that Hayakawa was not now nor had he ever been a member of the Japanese community in the Bay Area.

The press was another target of the students. We found repeatedly that many refused to talk to us until they perceived that we were sociologists, not reporters. One said, "The press is hovering around the administration building like a bunch of vultures waiting for some poor kid or some cop to get his head bashed in so they can film the blood and gore in living color." Almost all the students we talked to claimed that they could neither recognize the incidents they had witnessed nor the issues at stake from reading the newspapers, watching TV or reading weekly newsmagazines like *Time.* One student, who worked with a national TV technical crew, said that the sensationalism of the press was the fault not of the reporters on the scene but of their editors, who had a greater stake in boosting circulation and Nielson ratings than in informing the public.

The Huntley-Brinkley Report's TV film coverage came under special attack a number of times, while the *San Francisco Chronicle* was praised for some of its attempts to get beyond the superficial aspects of the strike—and condemned for printing a story of George Murray's inflammatory comments about the need for students to bring guns to campus and following it with a story about a Black Panther shoot-out with the police.

For many of the students, the incidents at San Francisco State have provided a first-hand opportunity to test both the veracity and competence of the press. Like so many other facets of the society that students are examining critically, the press has often been found wanting. And this explains why they care so little about public opinion about the strike: Public opinion, to them, is based upon the misinformation of the mass media. In short, Hayakawa may be impressed with the volume of his favorable mail, but the students are not.

Even the more moderate (but striking) students see the college as simply part of a larger set of agencies of social control—the Establishment. Their dissatisfactions with the college are usually expressed in terms of their general disapproval of society. Society (and State) is racist, corrupt, morally bankrupt, unresponsive to the needs of the oppressed. These students feel that they can and must do something about the situation they see confronting the nation, and at the same time they distrust the conventional political system.

Theoretical work by William A. Gamson, and empirical evidence from Detroit and Newark ghetto rioters collected and analyzed by Jeffery Paige, suggests that high sense of power and low political trust occurring together are major determinants of revolutionary behavior. And research by James McEvoy suggests that the same pattern of beliefs existed among early supporters of Senator Goldwater in 1964.

The students at San Francisco State, Columbia, Berkeley, Wisconsin, and other campuses on which dissent has exploded into confrontation have seen no further need to "work through channels." And it is true that too often the channels open to students within America's colleges have been shams. In the years when *in loco parentis* held sway, student politics were orderly, low-interest, and low-yield simulations of the procedures of democratic government outlined in the American government textbooks. This pattern of control began to crumble. after World War II. Students were no longer exclusively drawn from homogeneous age cohorts with little sophistication. Faculty and administrators, aroused by the same concerns as the students and having relatively great autonomy from the larger society, encouraged their charges—now increasingly defined as friends and co-equals. New status hierarchies emerged. Instead of news of the football team's practice sessions, the college papers were reporting the political activities of fellow students. Football players, confronted by smart Jewish boys from the Bronx or the South Side, found that, in the words of a recent anti-draft poster, girls said Yes to boys who said No—no to Wallace, to Goldwater, to Bull Conner, to Lyndon Johnson. This was a change that immeasurably increased the students' sense of political power.

During this same general period (1945-1968), American Negroes were experiencing a re-definition of their status in the society. A significant number of younger blacks developed an increasing sense of political power. Donald R. Matthews and James N. Prothro's studies of Southern Negro students show that political activism among black students was highly approved of by their black peers; the activists also got support from white liberal students in the North and from the white liberal community. Eventually, they heard the President of the United States say, in his Texas drawl, "We shall overcome."

Gradually, as blacks' levels of dissent rose, the American college acted to try to ameliorate the blacks' level of deprivation, especially by admitting academically unqualified Negroes. Everything that was done to ensure the success of these new students was also highly conducive to persuading them that the university was unlike anything they had ever encountered before: It was responsive, it was protective, and it offered almost unlimited moral, social, and financial support. Under these conditions, the expectations of the black students were raised. Their sense of power grew; they began to believe that they had a measure of control over their own destiny.

Until the war in Vietnam became the central political issue of the nation, the coalition of faculty, administrators, and black and white student activists was fairly stable. Trust was high; black students and white radicals, while militant in some cases, were not yet revolutionary. By the end of 1968, trust nearly disappeared from the campus at State and, we expect, from many other campuses as well.

Students everywhere viewed America's intervention in the war as a hideous manifestation of the values they felt were most responsible for the social problems of the 1960s. And the war, unlike the racism that had been the focus of student activism in the late 50s and early 60s, made its way into the campus in very tangible ways. Besides, to the students opposing the war, the collusion of the universities was seen in Selective Service regulations of student deferments and the revocation of these deferments for dissent, military recruiting, corporate recruiting by Dow and other military suppliers, and, of course, the fact that the Pentagon has traditionally drawn upon the academic community.

Like the American colonists' response to the imposition of the Stamp Act, the students began to rebel against the colleges when college officials feverishly tried to protect the "rights of the university" to keep its war-related research funds, to continue supplying students' grades to the Selective Service System, and to let students have freedom of choice in choosing an employer—even if the employer made napalm. These "rights" of course, had to be created to protect important professors and the research funds, and to show that colleges and universities were not subversive. The McCarthy era was probably still fresh in the minds of many academic bureaucrats as they pondered the fate of a state- or federally-supported school that openly defied the government by yielding to student demands on the war. That students, whose expectations of success were at a new high, should rebel in the face of this posture of the college is hardly surprising.

One major effect of the rebellion at State appears to be forthcoming in the form of punitive budgetary cuts by the Governor and the state legislature. Reagan has announced that "There will be no new programs" at either the state colleges or universities for 1969-1970, and it seems likely that additional sanctions will be imposed. In our judgment, they will further exacerbate the situation—in some cases, by radicalizing the faculty.

The outcome of the situation at State will also have important consequences for black and white militants and the movements they represent. If the administration yields to all the immediate demands of the militants, they will have won an important point—the belief that they can confront the Establishment and win. Unfortunately, it is clear that the use of force by student militants is generating an immensely hostile public, and this may well result in the election of officials committed, even more strongly than, say, Mayor Daley, to the repression of dissent of all types. If this occurs, at least in California we look forward to a crisis in the universities and colleges that will result in the loss of academic freedom, of political autonomy, and even, perhaps, of the constitutional rights of students and faculty in state-controlled institutions of higher education.

San Francisco State opens its second semester today. During the post-Christmas period of the first semester we visited the campus again and found that although final exams were taken by about 75 percent of the students, the campus was largely deserted in the weeks before exams. The American Federation of Teachers strike, finally approved by the San Francisco Labor Council late in December, was continuing, although some members apparently were leaving the picket line and returning to their classes as the second semester began. Avoiding automatic dismissal by teaching at least once in five days, the A.F.T. teachers represent the quarter of the faculty substantially committed to the strike.

Violence shifted from State to Berkeley during the examination break. We saw a number of strikers from State manning picket lines at Berkeley after the T.W.L.F. and the B.S.U. called a strike there. Support from State "volunteers" probably helped the Berkeley strikers give the impression of having large-scale support in the face of widespread apathy and antagonism from Berkeley faculty and students. Roger Heynes, Berkeley's chancellor, had acted long ago to implement black studies, but the B.S.U. and the T.W.L.F. ignored this and his behavior during the strike, in an attempt to gather support by damning his "racist" administration.

The budgets of the universities and the state colleges in California, as in the past three years, have been drastically cut from the amounts recommended by the schools' governing bodies. Hayakawa, Dumke, and university officials have all pleaded for more support for the colleges; we doubt that any will be forthcoming.

Saturday night, February 15, a powerful bomb was placed near the entrance to the Administration Building at State. Its explosion, heard for miles, blew out windows in the building but bad placement probably prevented serious damage. Earlier the same week, Hayakawa attempted to address the faculty in a meeting that traditionally takes place at the beginning of each semester. He was shouted down by Hare (then designated to be the head of the black studies department at State) and a number of other black faculty and administrators. When Hare and three other hecklers jumped on the stage and approached Hayakawa, they were arrested. Only about a third of State's faculty attended this meeting, an indication, we believe, of widespread faculty disaffection with Hayakawa. Hare is no longer going to head the black studies program.

San Francisco State is not a viable educational institution.

Some of its best faculty are leaving. Distrust is high. Deans and counselors who normally serve as advisers sit idle at their desks. Education may be continuing as a shrunken bureaucratic ritual, but the intangible sinew and spirit that bind an educational community together are absent.

Office doors wear signs instructing students where classes will meet off campus, how striking students can get grades, and when striking teachers will hold "office hours" on the picket line. Some department offices are decorated with huge anti-Hayakawa signs. Many faculty, not on strike, are anti-Hayakawa, antiviolence, antimilitancy, and hold their classes off campus, hoping to serve as moderators if and when San Francisco State returns to the business of learning.

Hayakawa claims victory. The school is physically open. The militants claim victory. The school has, for all practical purposes, been shut down. The majority caught between these antagonistic forces may well be asking, "Was it all worth it?" The militants, whose preferred means of social change is destruction, and the authorities, who for too long have been insensitive to social change, would do well to ponder the question.

March 1969

Confrontation
At Cornell

WILLIAM H. FRIEDLAND/HARRY EDWARDS

Bandoliers across their shoulders, rifles and shotguns casually held ready, the black students of Cornell broke into American consciousness one morning last April like an advance patrol of that army of barbarians which is the special nightmare of the affluent and, for some, their dream of regeneration. In that moment, fear—which everyone on the campus, both black and white, had known for days—rippled out and touched everyone.

Cornell seems an unlikely, not to say preposterous setting for such an event. Tucked away in rural upstate New York, the college until recently was comfortably settled in an atmosphere of genteel WASPishness. There was also an Ivy League rah-rah spirit about the place which only partially obscured the substantial number of lower-class youths who came to Ithaca under State University auspices to study agriculture, education and home economics. True, there had been a riot in 1958 (memorialized in Richard Farina's novel *Been Down So Long It Looks Like Up to Me*) over the right of students to have mixed parties without chaperons. But *political* activism came late to Cornell.

The trigger was pulled at Berkeley in 1964. After that, Cornell students began to organize themselves, somewhat feebly, into a group called Students For Education. SFE, before being washed away by the Vietnam escalation of 1965, brought into being a good many study commissions and some small changes, among them the conversion of the campus bookstore into a bookstore rather than a purveyor of required texts, setting up an on-campus coffee house, and some very limited changes in the grading system.

But as the Vietnam war went on and was intensified, students at Cornell, like those elsewhere, stepped up their protests. One major confrontation took place during an ROTC review in the college's cavernous Barton Hall, which later figured so importantly in the events of the Spring. Throughout this period, most student activism revolved around the Students for a Democratic Society. Like SDS everywhere, the Cornell group was anti-organizational, anti-leadership, using consensus decision-making procedures, committed to spontaneity. Despite this (or because of it), SDS has been remarkably efficient in mobilizing on the part of the students and a few faculty members

Until recently, the number of blacks at Cornell has been negligible. Indeed, into the early 1960's, those from outside the United States were far more numerous than American blacks. Furthermore, as at most American universities, the atmosphere at Cornell was almost unashamedly racist. Many fraternities, for example, constitutionally denied membership to non-Caucasians. But as the civil rights movement gathered force in the country, Cornell's liberals began to put pressure on the restrictive practices of the fraternities and tried to eliminate discrimination in off-campus housing. And Cornell students were among those who participated in the Freedom Summer of 1964, working on voter registration in Fayette County, Tennessee.

White involvement in civil rights activities fell off in 1965 however. The development of racial consciousness among blacks led to the belief that blacks had to make their own way and shed themselves of their white supporters if their movement was to be their own. Then, too, the escalation of the Vietnam war increasingly provided a focus for liberal and radical whites. At the same time, more significant changes were taking place at Cornell as the number of American black students began to increase. A Committee on Special Educational Projects (COSEP) was set up to locate and recruit black students and provide them with financial and other support. COSEP's success, while small, was such that by September 1968 there were 240 blacks at Cornell in a total of some 13,200.

But even before then, the presence of black students was causing considerable strain in the university. The separatist issue broke into the open when a black girl, living in the girls' dorms, experienced difficulties with her dormmates. The girl was referred to Cornell's clinic for psychiatric assistance and apparently found little sympathy there. Ordered to leave Cornell, she refused. This precipitated a crisis out of which came demands for separate housing so that blacks could be free of the pressures of living in a hostile environment. Reluctantly, the college made arrangements to establish several black co-ops.

Later, academic freedom seemed to many to be called into question when black students and others became convinced that a visiting professor was teaching racism. After complaining to every relevant agency of the university and being put off time after time, the blacks confronted the professor with the demand that he read a statement in class. When he insisted on reading it in advance and the blacks rejected this, he dismissed the class. The blacks thereupon sat in at the professor's department offices, holding the department chairman in his office.

On that same day occurred the assassination of Martin Luther King and the two events provided the university community with a rarely experienced shock. In addition, several fires were set and later, blacks used Cornell's memorial service to King as an opportunity to attack the university and America's whites.

If nothing else, these events during the year 1967-68 indicated that the blacks at Cornell had layed a strong base for their organization which soon everyone would know as the Afro-American Society.

In response to events of the 1968 spring term, the university moved to set up an Afro-American studies program. Throughout the summer and fall a committee made up of nine faculty and administration members and eight black students met to work out the program. But in the second week of December the black students revolted against what they saw as stalling tactics. They demanded total control of the program and refused to cooperate any further with the existing committee. The same week, six members of the Afro-American Society forced three whites to leave their offices in a university building on Waite Avenue—a building that the administration had promised to the Afro-American studies program, and during the same affair a photographer for the *Cornell Daily Sun* was roughed up when he refused to turn over a film.

At the same time, however, covert negotiations between the black students and the administration continued over the demands for an autonomous black studies program, but little progress was made and the blacks saw this as another expression of Cornell's unwillingness to take their demands seriously. Consequently, one week before the Christmas recess, black students at Cornell staged a number of demonstrations. Groups of them marched around the quadrangles playing bongo drums, while another contingent entered the President's office with water pistols. They also pushed white students away from several tables in the student union and claimed them for themselves as "black tables." Another time, they carried hundreds of books from the library shelves to the checkout counters, and dumped them there as "irrelevant." They also went to the clinic and demanded treatment by a black physician. Despite their sometimes playful aspects, these demonstrations had an ugly and threatening undercurrent that left most whites tense. Nevertheless, the administration did move toward implementing a black studies program. Not all black demands were met, but a black was chosen to be acting director and compromises were worked out that made the program a degree-granting one. Another consequence was that the black students saw their demonstrations as part of a political program necessary to help them gain a meaningful education at Cornell.

Still, the faculty and administration response to the demonstrations had been hostile and the process of finding scapegoats upon whom retribution might be visited got underway. In January, six students were charged before the Student-Faculty Conduct Board. The decision with respect to these students was one of the important factors leading to the 1969 confrontation.

The disciplinary issues were complicated by what happened during a conference on apartheid sponsored by Cornell's Center for International Studies. The 25 speakers, of whom only three were black, were not greeted sympathetically by an audience composed for the most part of Afro-Americans, black Africans, and SDS supporters. The latter moved rapidly from verbal hostility to more openly disruptive interventions. At a meeting on the second evening of the conference, the blacks turned out en masse to challenge Cornell President James Perkins on university investments in South Africa. As Perkins was speaking, one black student grabbed him by the collar and pulled him from the podium. Perkins, badly shaken, left the room. The campus reaction to this incident was hardly in favor of the blacks, despite the fact that there was an increasing sentiment that Cornell's endowments should be free of the taint of apartheid.

Meanwhile, preliminary to the trial of the six members of the Afro-American Society before the Student-Faculty Conduct Board, the AAS was claiming that the demonstrations of December had been political acts for which the organization should be held responsible. Selection of a few members could only be regarded as victimization. Accordingly, the six refused to appear before the Conduct Board. Then followed a period in which the six students were verbally threatened with suspension if they failed to appear before the Board. When they didn't show up, letters were sent. In April, just before the events that brought Cornell into the headlines, an obscure clause was discovered that permitted the Conduct Board to take action without the black students being present. On April 18, the Conduct Board reprimanded three of the blacks, dismissed charges against two others, while the charge against the last student was dropped because of his departure from the university.

Throughout this period, campus groups had been enunciating principles to support their positions on the issues involved. For the Conduct Board (and implicitly for the faculty and much of the student body) the issue raised was: Is the university a single community? If it is *a* community, must all "citizens" adhere to its rules? The blacks not only challenged the idea of *a* community but put forward the principle that no man should be judged except by a jury of his peers. The blacks also challenged the legitimacy of the Board, contending it was not a voluntary product of the campus community but one imposed by the racist apparatus of American society. In partial justification of their statement, the Afro-Americans pointed out that there was no black representation on the Board. A second conflict of principle arose over the issue of how personal, in contrast to political, acts could be judged. Some university groups argued that individuals rather than organizations had to be held responsible for their acts; organizations could not be tried before the Conduct Board. The blacks asserted the reverse was true: their actions were political, therefore their responsibility was collective. The blacks also argued that the university was not only the aggrieved party but the judge and jury as well, and principles of Anglo-Saxon justice declared that this should not be done. The Afro-American Society suggested that "arbitration" as in industrial-relations might be the appropriate model for a resolution of the problem.

In addition to the disciplinary issue, a number of other questions were deeply troubling to numbers of both students and faculty. During their seizure of the Waite Avenue building the blacks had insisted that their demands for an Afro-American studies program were "nonnegotiable." This was pure rhetoric, negotiations were going on through intermediaries, and most people knew it. Nevertheless, many faculty members interpreted the position of the blacks as needlessly intransigent. The black separatism issue had not gone down well with much of the university community either, especially those tables in the student union which had been claimed as black territory. Blacks moved around the campus in groups and were never found fraternizing with whites. This was upsetting to most faculty and students.

While attention centered on the blacks during the spring, a host of other issues affected large numbers of white students. SDS had made demands that the university provide housing not only for students but for the Ithaca community. Arguing that Cornell had thrown the burden of housing upon the community, SDS insisted that the university provide low-cost housing units for underprivileged groups in Ithaca. This issue generated considerable support in faculty and student circles: a network of housing organizations was created to bring pressures for a university commitment. A second issue burgeoned over the impending departure of several noted historians and humanities professors. Humanities has not been strong at Cornell; it is not an area to which the administration has paid any serious attention. So the issue was one that mobilized many Arts and Sciences students. Still other grievances were those of graduate assistants over financial support, and Cornell's South African investments. And, in mid-April, just before the confrontation, a popular sociology professor, one of the first winners of a teaching award, was refused tenure because of his weak publication record.

These issues, and others, created an atmosphere of tension that threatened to come to a crisis on Wednesday, March 12, when the university faculty was scheduled to meet. But when the day came, the faculty adopted a resolution supporting the integrity of the adjudicatory machinery of the Conduct Board and the situation continued to bubble with neither confrontation nor resolution.

At 3:00 A.M. on the morning of Friday, April 18, persons still unknown threw a burning cross on the porch of the black girls' co-operative. Responding to a call, the campus safety patrol reached the co-op where the fire was stamped out. What exactly the campus safety patrol did at the scene of the cross-burning is not clear, but apparently all seven officers covering the incident withdrew, ostensibly on other business, leaving no protection at the co-op. Much later, a guard was established, but by that time the blacks had evidently lost any confidence they may have had in campus protection. This was to be exacerbated as campus officials, while strongly deploring the incident, referred to it as a "thoughtless prank." To the blacks, the symbolism of the event was as powerful as if someone had burned a *Mogen David* in front of a Jewish fraternity. Had such a thing occurred, the blacks reasoned, all the powers of the university would have been brought to bear and the cries of outrage would have been mighty indeed. As it was, the somewhat cavalier attitudes of the university seemed still another reflection of institutional racism, less open perhaps than the occasional group of white boys who had shouted "nigger" at black girls, but racism it was, nevertheless.

As word of the cross-burning spread among the blacks, they assembled at the co-op to decide what action was necessary to protect their women. The defense of their own kind, this was to become a central symbol of the events that followed. As for their choice of target—the student union at Willard Straight Hall, this was in part dictated by the dramatic possibilities implicit in the fact that Parents' Weekend had begun and the opportunity to demonstrate before thousands of parents was tactically so tempting that rumors had been circulating that some group would seize some building somewhere regardless of the issue. How significant a role the rumors played in the deliberations of the blacks is not known, but the tactical impact of the seizure was clear. But it is clear that in deciding to take over the student union, the blacks were intent only on giving an emphatic warning to the campus to "get off our backs," they were not concerned with specific demands. Indeed, the original intent was to seize the building for one day only and then surrender it peaceably.

At 6:00 A.M. on Saturday, April 19, the blacks marched into Willard Straight Hall, calmly ordered service personnel preparing for the day's activities to remove themselves, expelled from guest rooms in the loft a number of visiting parents, and locked up the building.

News of the seizure soon spread throughout the campus; by 8:00 A.M. everyone knew the university was on the brink of another confrontation. For many of the students, particularly those at either end of the political spectrum, having an audience of parents probably served as a stimulus to action. The conservative students tend to be concentrated in a small number of houses that remain "lily-white" and in the fraternities. One of these, Delta Upsilon, is known as the "jock house," because of its unusual number of athletes. It is also one of the most WASPish houses and at present includes no Negro members. Around 9:00 in the morning, about 15 to 20 DU members attempted to break into Straight Hall, and some eight or nine succeeded in getting in before a group of SDS people prevented the rest from entering. While a good deal of pushing, shoving, and arguing was going on outside, inside there was a brief but violent battle between the blacks and the DU men. Three whites and one black were injured, no one seriously. The battle ended with the expulsion of the fraternity boys, but the blacks, even though badly shaken, announced that any other attack would be met by mounting escalation of force. SDS members, standing outside in sympathy with the blacks, rejected a proposal to seize another building and maintained a picket around the entire building to show their support.

The DU attack can be, and was, interpreted in various ways. But from the viewpoint of the blacks, it represented a university attempt to oust them from the building. The campus patrol was supposed to have been guarding the building to prevent entry. Therefore, the fact that the DU people had gotten in was all too easily understood by the blacks as administrative complicity, rather than what it probably was—a spontaneous, self-organized attempt by frat boys. For their part, the DU men insisted that they had entered the building to engage in discussion with black athletes inside and that there was no intent to recapture the building. (There is no evidence, however, that there were ever any black athletes involved in the seizure of the student union.) The DU men claimed that they went in empty-handed; the blacks insisted that they came in with clubs.

Following this incident, the campus gave itself up to an orgy of rumors. Throughout the day, it was circulated about that armed vigilante groups were preparing to mount an attack on Straight Hall. Inside the Hall, the blacks received continuous telephone messages about these vigilantes. By Saturday afternoon, according to the testimony of the blacks and the administrators in telephone contact with them, the occupiers were in a state of terrible tension. It was then that they decided to bring in guns to protect themselves. In the end, they were to have 13 rifles, and two shotguns.

Saturday night passed quietly, but the tension throughout the campus was approaching a critical point. By Sunday morning, Cornell administrators had decided that it would be necessary to end the occupation of the Straight at almost any cost.

That the occupation of the Straight was a precipitous act, probably triggered by the cross-burning, is attested to, first, by the lengthy time it took the blacks to formulate demands; and, second, the relatively flimsy nature of the demands. By Saturday afternoon, three had emerged from Willard Straight, of which one was subsequently withdrawn. The first demand called for a nullification of the three reprimands handed down by the Conduct Committee after the demonstrations of December; the second called for a full investigation and report of the Afro-American Society of the cross-burning incident. That the blacks would take such very serious steps for such tired and modest demands indicates their state of fear and tension. But this was never communicated to the campus, except to those in the administration, Dean Robert Miller especially, who were in direct contact with them. With the latter, the blacks entered into a six-point agreement to end the Straight occupation. It included a commitment to call a full faculty meeting and recommend that the reprimands be declared null and void.

However, the occupiers of Straight Hall were still determined to demonstrate to Cornell whites that they were no longer sitting ducks. So it was that despite pressure from administrators for a decorous exit, the blacks proceeded to make a dramatic exit, brandishing their weapons. It soon became convenient for the shocked white majority of the university to look upon this as a new escalation in student activism; while campus after campus had experienced confrontation, it was argued that this was the first time that students had taken up guns. It was within this context that Cornell arrived at a new level of internal tension on Monday, April 21.

The sight of armed students marching across their campus was too much for the overwhelming majority of the faculty. Unable to understand, or ignorant of, the black students' side of the story, their immediate reaction on

Monday, April 21, was one of bitter hostility to any compromise or accommodation of black demands. Their antagonism focused on the six-point agreement reached between the administration and the blacks. Some forty members of the faculty, largely in the government and history departments, signed a statement declaring they would resign if the reprimands were nullified at the Monday faculty meeting.

Tension increased during the day as the opposition to nullification crystallized in the faculty. What the reaction of the blacks would be to a refusal to nullify was unclear, but there was an unspoken and widespread fear that Cornell might be headed toward some kind of shoot-out. In these circumstances, President Perkins called a convocation in Barton Hall just before the university faculty meeting. Some 10,000 students, faculty and staff assembled to hear an innocuous 20-minute statement by the President that left issues more undefined than before. There had been an expectation that presidential leadership was to be asserted.

Instead, in an atmosphere of diffuse fear and anger, in which the focused hostility of the government and history departments stood out, the faculty assembled at 4:00 P.M. in unprecedented numbers. The meeting began with a report by Dean of the Faculty, Robert Miller, who introduced a formal motion calling for nullification of the reprimands. The Dean's assessment was that the danger to human life at Cornell was real and had to be avoided even at the cost of failing to sustain the authority of the adjudicatory machinery, the Conduct Board. This approach was rejected by the faculty. Instead, they voted a substitute motion that upheld the legitimacy of the adjudicatory machinery and took no action on the nullification of the reprimands. Continuing for over four hours of intricate parliamentary maneuvers, the faculty meeting showed that the majority was adamantly opposed to nullification, but there was also an obdurate, vocal minority supporting the blacks or concerned with the consequences of refusal to nullify. President Perkins had little political capital at this meeting despite his earlier proclamation of limited emergency, a statement that anyone carrying guns on university property would be suspended summarily, or that disruptive demonstrations would lead to immediate suspensions. Nevertheless, he was able to achieve minimal consensus with a resolution calling for the initiation of discussions between the Faculty Council and the Afro-American Society and calling for another full faculty meeting.

Dean Miller now tendered his resignation, stating that by the refusal to vote on his motion, the faculty was repudiating his estimate of the situation. He was promptly given a standing ovation, which neatly illustrated the faculty's dilemma. They respected him and wanted peace, but they felt they had to refuse to make concessions under what they saw as the threat of armed coercion. As the meeting ended at 8:15 and the faculty departed for long-delayed dinners, there was the sense that no solution had been found and that the campus was entering a new and more dangerous situation.

On Monday evening SDS called a meeting attended by 2,500, but it ended inconclusively. SDS was waiting for the blacks.

By Tuesday morning the campus was in chaos. Many classes did not meet, and in those that did the only topics were those raised by the confrontation. The university leadership, seeking desperately to remedy a deteriorating situation, consulted the deans of the colleges and proposed meetings of college faculties and the beginning of a broad-based discussion at all levels. The intent was to structure free-floating campus anxieties into organized meetings geared to a search for solutions. In the leadership vacuum created by the conflict between the administration's willingness to make concessions and an obdurate faculty, the administration sought only to keep a dialogue going. The fear of bloodshed was everywhere.

At noon, an ephemeral organization named "The Concerned Faculty," consisting largely of elements supporting the blacks, convened for several hours. Urged on by members of the Afro-American Society, "The Concerned Faculty" were unable to decide on anything more than gestures of solidarity. Twenty-six of those attending agreed to seize a building if necessary, while some 60-odd announced their willingness to strike.

Meanwhile, however, at meetings of the faculties of the various colleges, an apparent change in campus opinion began to be felt. The colleges of Arts and Sciences and Home Economics voted to recommend nullification of the Conduct Board's reprimands, and at its 7:00 P.M. meeting, the Faculty Council did the same, while calling for another meeting of the faculty for Wednesday noon. But several other faculties were still determined to maintain business as usual.

That same Tuesday, student opinion on campus began crystallizing around a call by SDS and the Inter-Fraternity Council for a teach-in at Barton Hall, the largest building on campus. By early evening, thousands of students had begun moving to the Hall. Like the faculty, they too seemed intent on avoiding violence between the blacks and other forces. Somewhere between 8,000 to 10,000 people gathered there and as the evening went on, a consensus emerged that it was vital for Cornell students to remain in the building and act as a pressure group on the Cornell faculty, which was scheduled to meet the next day, Wednesday, April 23. SDS speakers proposed that the students declare that they had seized the building, thereby defying President Perkins' new regulation prohibiting such actions. Only a handful objected, and later in the evening Perkins condoned the occupation of Barton Hall, though he persisted in defining it as a teach-in rather than as the seizure the students had declared it to be. This "legal" anomaly continued through the night. Thousands made preparations for the all-night meeting; a collection was taken and soon sandwiches and drinks were being passed out among the teeming mass of students.

As the evening of Tuesday, April 22 wore on, students organized according to their colleges to lobby faculty members for their vote on Wednesday. Around the edges of the Hall, there were dozens of meetings involving tens and hundreds of students. At 3:00 A.M. meetings were still continuing; they included not only groups from different colleges, but various ad hoc committees on the press, particularly the *Sun,* the university's student operated newspaper. One large group of biology students was attempting to deal with the problem of a professor who refused to cancel a quiz scheduled for the next day. The mood in Barton Hall was tensely hopeful; that such an incredible outpouring of students could take place showed that student sentiment had shifted to the blacks, although it was less clear whether the shift had occurred for substantive reasons or because of the fear of violence.

On Wednesday, April 23, the students were wakened by a banjo ensemble and the speech-making began again in the Hall. Elsewhere on the campus, hundreds of meetings were taking place as faculty members were visited by student lobbyists.

Soon after the faculty meeting was gavelled into session by Provost Dale Corson, it became evident that a clear shift had occurred among the members. Despite hardline speeches by government and history faculty members, a motion to nullify was replaced by a second motion which not only called for nullification but also for restructuring the university. The substitute was introduced by Professor Clinton Rossiter who had signed, only two days before, the statement threatening resignation if the reprimands were nullified. Biology professor William Keaton explained how a large delegation of his students from Barton Hall had asked him to change his vote, not because of the threat of violence, but because they wanted him to have faith in them. But the probable major reason for the shift was expressed by Nobel physicist, Hans Bethe, who said that since the moderates were moving toward the SDS left, it was necessary for the faculty to reverse itself to occupy the middle ground and isolate radicals. The resolution calling for nullification and restructuring the university carried by a voice vote probably on the order of three or four to one. The faculty now accepted a resolution by philosopher Max Black informing the students "We hear you. . . ."

A thousand faculty members then moved to Barton Hall where they received a standing ovation. The faculty action demonstrated to the students the latter's influence on the decision-making process; from this point, emphasis shifted to the second part of the Rossiter resolution on restructuring the university.

As the faculty arrived, Eric Evans, vice president of the Afro-American Society was talking. President Perkins came to the podium where, according to Evans, he put his arm around him, smiled in fatherly fashion, and said "Sit down, I want to talk." Evans refused to surrender the microphone. Nothing better demonstrated the students' new mood than the hilarious cheering that broke out when Evans informed them of this exchange. While Perkins fidgeted uncomfortably on the floor with the students and faculty, Evans continued a leisurely review of events leading up to the Willard Straight seizure. When he finished, Perkins spoke and was followed by a succession of others. Slowly the Barton Hall meeting achieved a catharsis from the tensions of the past five days. By 5:00 P.M. the teach-in had ended. Cornell now entered a new phase ostensibly dedicated to a restructuring of the university.

The period immediately following the Barton Hall catharsis was characterized by what can only be called organizational withdrawal symptoms. The most dramatic occurred within SDS which either could not or would not come to grips with its lack of organization and need for leadership. The faculty, too, lost the capacity to function coherently as a corporate body. The Afro-Americans managed to rename themselves the Black Liberation Front but otherwise they also retreated into themselves to try to decide how to relate to the college community under the new circumstances.

Administration officials and traditionally apathetic students also withdrew. The administration was in a state of shock; all that emerged from Day Hall, the administration building, were generalized statements reinforcing previous statements about guns and disruptive demonstrations. Beyond that, Day Hall demonstrated no capacity to provide any structure, guidance, or direction. As for the students, once catharsis had been achieved on Wednesday they lost the capacity to act.

In these circumstances, the tendency was to revert to the traditional, though weakened, institutional structure. Students and faculty turned to colleges and departments, that is, to more manageable social units. With this, the cooling-off process began. It was not that everyone's behavior was as in the past, but students once again came into direct face-to-face relations with teachers, to whom they had always exhibited deference. In a (crude) word, the "reniggerization" of the students had begun.

But the cooling-off took time. It was a week before student statements became more qualified and less concrete and hard-line. Faculty statements, too, became tougher as the teachers reverted to traditional issues of teaching vs. research, academic freedom, and the like.

What this means is that any action with respect to change in university structure, functioning, and priorities will be based on traditional university norms and values. Moreover, the summer will be used as a cooling-off period. Once again there will be the gradual accretion of "data," the rational consideration of infinitesimal details. This does not mean that the faculty will be unwilling to change at all; rather that change will be oriented toward maintaining basic structures. Cooptation of student dissidents will become the major mechanicism for attempting to alleviate pressure, for it is evident that the major emphasis is now on alleviating pressure, not solving problems. More fundamental commitment to change in the governance of the university or the educational process remains small.

In the weeks following the adjournment of Barton Hall, the administration, the students, and the faculty have been inadvertently laying the foundation for the next confrontation by reversion to old structures.

But first, it is perhaps worth a short digression to examine why so few black students at Cornell have been able to create such enormous pressures (and we limit ourselves to Cornell here, although some of this analysis is appropriate to black-student experience at other universities).

There is, first of all, a reservoir of readily exploitable guilt in liberal academic circles, but much more depends upon the social situation of a relatively small number of blacks resident in an overwhelmingly white university. All students experience adaptation and living problems in residential universities. Thrown together for long periods of intensive community living and having to navigate a host of curricular and extracurricular problems and opportunities, most students have to find ways of making it all manageable.

As blacks increased at Cornell they experienced the usual problems that blacks undergo in a white environment. But the present generation of black collegians entered the university just as black-power ideology began to affect black intellectuals. This, and the antipathy they felt on the part of the whites, led black students into closer and more intensive relations with each other. The coalescence was further intensified by such incidents as that of whites yelling "nigger" at black girls. Each incident was stored away and became the subject of continual discussion. In these circumstances, black students began to act against their environment and their number was exactly right for the maximum cohesiveness needed to generate pressures. If larger number of blacks were present, this cohesiveness would be difficult, if not impossible.

But the main grounds on which we would predict further troubles for Cornell are the discrepancies between student hopes for change and the structural inabilities of universities to obtain significant change, especially in the educational process. This will create serious problems because the demand of students for restructuring the learning process remains unresolved. At the same time, the social conditions contributing to this demand also remain unresolved: poverty, discrimination, racism, the war in Vietnam, continue and are interpreted, probably correctly, as worsening. Most students are naive in that they think university reform will take place by itself, and many believe that something tangible will come out of Barton Hall. As students realize that little or nothing can emerge, they will find themselves increasingly frustrated.

The specific issue that will trigger the next action can come from a variety of sources: recruitment by employers (which most universities will not eliminate because a majority of students want it), pressures for open recruitment of blacks or other deprivileged groups, financial shortages as alumni react against campus actions, relations with the surrounding community, university investments, and so on. Thus, the institutional inabilities to change rapidly and drastically practically guarantee new confrontations in the next academic year at Cornell.

June 1969

The Phantom Racist

RITA JAMES SIMON/JAMES CAREY

In 1963 three freshmen Negro athletes at the University of Illinois at Urbana sought out a Negro graduate student and complained to him about racial discrimination against them. Specifically, they said, a member of the football staff had urged them to stop dating or being seen with white girls. The Negro graduate student arranged for the athletes to sign affidavits charging the Athletic Association, which administers inter-collegiate athletics at Illinois, with discrimination.

This was the precipitating incident in the search for what we call the "phantom racist." He is a phantom because the specific charges of discrimination were never proven, but neither were the issues he raised ever resolved. They underscore the continuing problems of Negro students at the university.

First, some background about the University of Illinois must be considered:

■ There are approximately 350 Negro students at the University of Illinois. The estimated number is surprisingly small considering that nearby Chicago has the second largest Negro population in the United States. Negroes are approximately one percent of the university enrollment.

■ Among the 350, about 35 have athletic scholarships. While athletes must meet minimum standards of academic achievement, they are chosen principally for athletic ability.

■ Few Negro students at the University of Illinois are active in civil rights organizations or have participated in civil rights demonstrations. Some went South to serve in the Mississippi summer projects and voter registration drives but few have taken action directly focused on campus and community conditions. Civil rights groups made attempts to end "white only" membership in fraternities and sororities and to end discrimination in privately owned rooming houses. (These demands were met when the university set a date for the removal of discriminatory clauses and required non-discrimination from any landlord renting to university students after January 1, 1966.)

■ Independent studies have indicated that Negroes, in general, do not consider the university or its environs as a congenial place for them.

After the complaint of discrimination was made in 1963, the following sequence of events occurred.

Armed with the affidavits from the three freshmen athletes, a group of graduate students, most of them Negro and members of the campus chapter of the NAACP, formed an *ad hoc* committee of Students for Human Dignity and Social Peace. The committee approached the *Daily Illini,* the student undergraduate paper, and asked to have the charges of discrimination publicized. The editor of the *Daily Illini* doubted the charges and delayed printing them. Word of the committees attempts leaked to the Athletic Association and to other Negro athletes, who had not been informed.

One football player, a self-appointed spokesman for the other Negro athletes, contacted the *Daily Illini* editor and certain members of the *ad hoc* committee. The athlete disputed the charges and threatened to discredit them and the *ad hoc* committee if the Athlete Association and the coaching staff were harmed. He contended that if the athletes were warned about dating it was because their class work was suffering and the coach was merely trying to help them. He pointed out that a large number of Negro athletes dated white girls and received no warning from the coaches.

Members of the *ad hoc* committee, in a subsequent interview, said that the coach was responding to pressure from the town, which found the sight of Negro boys and white girls together repugnant and that talking to the athletes about their social life was *prima facie* evidence of discrimination.

After some deliberation, the *Daily Illini* refused to run the story. Lacking support from the Negro athletes and the student daily, the *ad hoc* committee changed its strategy.

The *ad hoc* committee decided to gather additional evidence of the mistreatment of Negro athletes in particular and of Negro students in general. To that end the committee took testimony from Negro athletes for presentation to the university administration. The football player who had threatened to discredit the *ad hoc* committee was one of those who testified. This athlete later said his testimony was directed solely against the Department of Physical Education on the campus. The athletes did contend, however, that the University of Illinois was not a good school for Negroes; they said that the atmosphere was hostile and they had been humiliated by teachers, coaches, other athletes, and white students. They said that when they were used by the Athletic Association to recruit other Negro athletes, they had a difficult time, in good conscience, urging them to come. Much of their testimony was about the bad climate for Negro students in general—not just Negro athletes.

The evidence was presented to the university administration and to the all-university Committee on Race Relations in December of 1963. A sub-committee of the race relations committee investigated the Department of Physical Education and the Athletic Association. As a result, the provost issued a statement in September 1964 that did not specifically confirm the *ad hoc* committee charges, but did warn against discrimination against Negro athletes. It directed staff members to refrain from using racially demeaning expressions, to cease interference in the social activities of athletes, and to discourage white athletes from intruding into the private affairs of Negro athletes.

Members of the university administration later commented that they felt that the investigation had substantially improved the racial climate on the campus, that particularly objectionable practices had been stopped, and that the Negro students themselves were satisfied.

But following the close of the football season in 1964, members of the *ad hoc* committee received evidence that the provost's directive was being ignored. A Negro athlete confided to a Negro graduate student that he had been warned against interracial dating, and that his choice of courses was interfered with. At this time, the campus chapter of the NAACP entered the conflict in defense of the Negro athletes. Many members of the *ad hoc* committee had left the university and those who remained decided to turn over all of the committee's materials to the NAACP and have them continue where the committee left off. Distrustful of the administration and its motives, the NAACP took its case directly to the public.

Until January 1965, the conflict between Negro students

and the university had been a private matter. Persistent rumors had circulated but most of the faculty, students, and community were unaware of the conflict. The NAACP made the conflict a public matter by releasing to the press a resolution which charged:

> For the last several years complaints have been lodged with this office alleging that the University Athletic Association and members of the Physical Education Department including some coaches, have been guilty of racially discriminatory policies . . .
>
> A special committee, appointed by the President's office, found that many of the allegations were true . . .
>
> But the NAACP has learned that Negro athletes are still being subjected to such discriminatory practices.

The NAACP also sent approximately 40 letters to high schools throughout the nation urging Negro athletes not to come to the university.

Three days later a statement, claiming to represent the opinions of all Negro athletes on campus, was released to the news media. It denounced the NAACP and defended the coaches and the Athletic Association.

> We, the Negro athletes of the University of Illinois, do, without qualification, fully denounce recent allegations made by the University of Illinois chapter of the NAACP concerning alleged discrimination against university athletes.
>
> First, the Negro athlete on the University of Illinois campus is articulate, he is well aware of his position as an individual and as a member of the Negro race, he is, further, aware of his position as a member of a team which represents the U. of I. He does not need an organized spokesman, whether it be the NAACP or some other organization.
>
> Negro athletes at the University of Illinois feel their

civil rights have been violated by the NAACP in their failure to seek our counsel, both as a group and as individual citizens before taking the irresponsible action of attacking the U. of I. Athletic Association.

The day has long since passed when the philosophy of "protecting our little brown brother" is needed. The Negro athlete at the U. of I. is a student first. He is to receive an education at one of the nation's finest universities. He is not a shuffling, grinning "Uncle Tom" as the NAACP's action would indicate. . . .

We feel, moreover, that the national organization of the NAACP should publically censure the U. of I. chapter for their action.

We categorically deny the existence of any segregationalist measures on the part of any member of the U. of I. coaching staff.

In making this statement Negro athletes wish to make very clear that their remarks represent the opinions of EVERY Negro athlete, without exception.

Following the exchange of charges, other organizations and groups entered the conflict: the local chapter of the American Association of University Professors, the public relations office of the university, the provost's office, and many members of the faculty, fraternities, sororities, and student groups. Press and television coverage continued for almost three weeks.

The day after release of the resolution reportedly representing all Negro athletes, the NAACP stated:

We, the University of Illinois chapter of the NAACP, are disheartened, but not surprised, by the repudiation of our recently passed resolution purporting to speak for all of the Negro athletes, past and present. We do not choose to engage in any internecine debate with this group. However, we stand on our resolution.

Later the NAACP claimed to have affidavits describing specific discriminatory practices by certain coaches and professors. (None of these affidavits were ever made public.) Other campus organizations joined in support of the NAACP—the executive council of the Friends of SNCC, and two Negro sororities and fraternities.

A few days later the NAACP spokesmen charged that the athletes' statement denouncing them was a fraud. They claimed that the athletes never saw it before it appeared in print, and that it was the work and opinion of only one man—the athlete spokesman who in the past had both supported and denounced the university's policies. No one, they said—not even the athletes themselves—had ever seen a copy of the statement with the signature of all the Negro athletes on it. Even the director of public information at the university, who announced that 25 of the 27 Negro athletes on campus had attended a meeting and signed the statement, was unable to produce a signed copy for more than a month after it was released. When the statement was finally produced the NAACP charged that the signatures were obtained under duress, that it had taken the Athletic Association a month to get the athletes to sign.

The story was picked up by the national news services and publicized across the country. Sports columnists on both coasts commented on potential loss of athletes; national civil rights leaders deplored continuance of discrimination at the Illinois campus. Locally, the *Daily Illini* editorially bewailed the absence of information and continued suspicion and distrust.

And then, without formal charges ever being made, without identification of either the racist or the athletes, without resolution of the issues, without adjudication of the charges, the case dropped from public view. It left behind suspicion, consternation, and damaged reputations.

Acting independently, we attempted as researchers to determine what the facts were, to understand how the situation had become as confused as it was, and to unravel the snarled communications. We interviewed members of the NAACP, Negro athletes, and concerned members of the faculty, hoping to disentangle fact from fiction. Although partly successful in gathering facts, we could not resolve basic issues; and here lies much of the significance.

Our procedure was straightforward. We interviewed two officers of the NAACP (both Negro graduate students), and the author of the statement from the Negro athletes, a graduating senior on the football team. We read all published accounts and interpretations, talked with past and current faculty members close to the students involved. Most important of all, we interviewed, by anonymous questionnaire, 15 of the 27 Negro athletes at the university (nine of them had attended the meeting during which plans to publish a denunciation of the NAACP were supposedly formulated).

When the NAACP took the issue to the media, the case became part of the great public drama of civil rights. That is, the case became subject to the laws of drama rather than the laws of reason. Men had to cast themselves in roles appropriate to the drama—as gods and devils, racists, integrationists, or liberal fools. Because mass exposure makes celebrities overnight, vanity and ego got locked into the discussion. For example, as the charges and counter charges were hurled we became increasingly suspicious, on the basis of our interviews, that part of the trouble was caused by a personal vendetta between two Negroes—the leader of the athletes and one of the leaders of the NAACP.

Because the case of discrimination expressed much more than concern for a few athletes and because the media turned the case into a dramatic conflict, it became virtually impossible to resolve the issue, to interpret the events, or even to get a consistent rendering of the facts.

Some things did emerge clearly, however. The whole episode was precipitated by the complaint of a single Negro athlete. One of the NAACP officers revealed to us his name and the nature of his complaint.

But the NAACP refused to make any of this information public—because the athlete did not want it made public. He was *not* graduating and was fearful of retaliation. According to the NAACP, he had been told to stop dating white girls and had been pressured to major in physical education although he preferred to study something else and had already been accepted by the other school.

According to the NAACP, this complaint fit a pattern. The complaints investigated by the provost's office a year and a half earlier, also involved interference by the staff in the social activities of Negro athletes. The provost's directive of September 1964 had not been heeded.

Two questions still remained:

■ Why hadn't the NAACP reported the complaint to the university before it contacted the high school athletes and the press?

■ Why didn't the NAACP try to get endorsement from at least some of the Negro athletes—or at the very least inform them—before publicizing their resolution?

Our informants claimed that one member had talked to someone on the president's staff and was told that the NAACP should document the incident. Two other representatives of the NAACP then offered to bring the complaining student to testify directly if the administration would guarantee his immunity.

But, our informants said, the university refused to "promise anything"; also the university spokesmen played down the seriousness of the charge. The NAACP therefore felt that even if they did produce the student, the university would not take a serious view of the matter, and he might lose his athletic scholarship or be otherwise penalized. They believed that the university had not enforced its 1964 directive and could not be trusted now. (The university claims that such an encounter never took place; that casual mention had been made of a developing incident, but that none was ever specifically outlined, no charges ever made, and that the university at all times offered complete protection to any Negro wishing to protest.

As to the second question, in a sense the NAACP was acting as an unauthorized spokesman for the athletes. (A charge later leveled at the NAACP was that they ignored the athletes, because, to put it mildly, they looked down on them, considered them dull, unable to understand the issues, in need of defense by more intelligent and articulate Negroes.)

But the NAACP did not feel they needed endorsement —one case of discrimination, when discrimination clearly violates rules and official policy, is sufficient cause for complaint. They also believed that by leaving the athletes out, they were actually protecting their best interests. One put it this way:

They really would rather not get involved and this is quite understandable. If you are on a team no one wants to be caught in a controversy involving that particular party and his immediate superiors—his boss, in other words. That is what the relationship really amounts to.

The NAACP thus felt they were being sensitive to the conflicting demands on the Negro athletes and did not want to hinder their careers. But they also believed that they had the implicit support of the Negro athletes, that privately the athletes would applaud them. They had listened to the athletes complain many times about unfair and discriminatory practices, and of their helplessness to do anything about it as long as they wanted to play.

Our informants thought, therefore, that the athletes wanted and needed their help—even though, as one acknowledged, none of the Negro athletes were members of the NAACP.

The NAACP was surprised and angered when the statement reportedly signed by the Negro athletes was published. One said:

At first, after this thing broke and the resolution was released, I was very angry with all of them. I had heard these groups complain many times ever since last spring. Then they turn around and take a position like this. I was pretty angry and I decided that I would help the people that . . . wanted to be helped, and as for the other people, it's just too bad. If they want to be kicked around, they have that right. I just don't want them coming to me anymore saying what "the man" is doing to them.

But, he said he later found that the statement was "in fact the opinion of only one man." Two of the athletes who attended the meeting came to see him afterward and told him that the group had agreed upon a short statement which exonerated a few coaches and stated that as individuals they had not experienced discrimination by the Athletic Association. But that at no time did the athletes attack the NAACP nor deny the existence of discrimination by coaches.

So much for the NAACP's position. What of the other side? Did the athletes agree with the counter-resolution? Did they condemn the NAACP's action? We have two sources of information—our interview with the organizer and author of the statement and the responses of 15 other Negro athletes to an anonymous questionnaire.

The author said he believed that "the coach (Pete Elliot) and his staff did not use discriminatory practices and that the NAACP's attack on the staff as a whole was unjustified and untrue." As soon as he read the NAACP's resolution in the newspaper on Friday (the first he knew of it), he phoned Elliot to apologize and to express his loyalty to him. During the conversation he told Elliot that he was pretty sure the other Negro athletes agreed, and he would find out by calling a meeting. On Sunday evening, the local radio and television stations announced and read in full the resolution expressing the sentiment of the Negro athletes against the NAACP. The author claims that it reflected accurately the opinions expressed during the meeting, and that most (although not all) athletes read and signed it before release. The only reason all did not sign was simply because he could not locate them in time; all had agreed that the resolution should be written and publicized.

At this point, the NAACP used this athlete's earlier words against him. A few months before he had taken part in a student discussion on the "impressions, attitudes, and feelings of the Negro athlete," and the tape-recording of this discussion had been presented to the administration as evidence of discrimination. Now his remarks were publicized by the NAACP. He had complained that at the Rose Bowl game the previous winter, a white all-American had called him a "black nigger." He said:

The thing that hurt me most was . . . the position the coaches took. The actual blame was placed on me. The coaches made an attempt to persuade the rest of the Negroes on the team that it was my fault and due to my nature; I was told that I should make a statement to try to soothe the feelings of the team. I didn't see what I could say to the team other than I was sorry he called me a black nigger. The issue was never really covered over. I think this is an example of the type of situation on our team. I think this is true in the administration. I think this is true in the various schools on campus, especially the school of Physical Education and I think that something has to be done. . . .

Now you ask me why I wouldn't recommend this type of school to another Negro student. . . .

I think the most disgraceful lack of administration here at the University of Illinois is that it is not geared at all for the Negro student. This is not just the athlete. . . .

The Negro athlete and the Negro student is completely without facilities; completely without anything to do unless we go to town or unless we go to some activities that are off-campus. . . .

The tape proved, as it was intended to, that the author was inconsistent. But that still does not answer the basic question: did the resolution published in the name of all the Negro athletes actually represent their views?

We decided to contact the athletes directly. It turned out that this was the most difficult and complicated task in the entire fact-finding operation. They were extremely loath to talk even when assured that no one would be quoted, and that we did not represent the university in this matter. We finally had to get the NAACP and the leading Negro athlete to act as intermediaries.

Of the 15 respondents (not including the author of the resolution, but including the original complainant to the NAACP) 14 answered that they disagreed with the NAACP statement. All 15 said they thought the NAACP should have talked with the Negro athletes before releasing the story—and 13 said the fact that they did not was important: "Everyone should have a chance to voice his own opinion"; "Athletes, Negro or white, aren't dumb. We can speak for ourselves"; "The statement isn't true." Some said "the NAACP challenged the maturity and intelligence of every Negro athlete on campus." All stated that they disapproved of the NAACP writing letters to Negro high school athletes.

On the other hand, only ten of the 15 athletes who filled out the questionnaire had actually attended the Sunday meeting. About half of the total respondents said they had seen the NAACP resolution and talked about it beforehand. When asked to describe what they understood the group had decided to do, nine of the ten who attended said "write a letter of rebuttal," or "go on record in defense of the Athletic Association" or "make up a statement in which each sport where there are Negro players individually clear that sport." One said "talk the situation over with the NAACP."

All but one claimed that everyone in the group went along with the decision to censure the NAACP publicly. Of the ten, seven said they saw and signed the statement later that evening. Two said they signed it several weeks later after they had seen it in print. One said he never signed it because he did not have the chance to. Three of the five who did not attend the meeting saw and signed the statement at a later time.

Only one of the respondents who attended the Sunday meeting believed that the statement did not reflect the group decision and he did not sign. He felt that the author's attack on the NAACP did not reflect either the group's or his own feeling. He wrote:

The NAACP is the strongest organization for Negroes. Why should I hurt them? I am not trying to help the Athletic Association by hurting the NAACP.

When asked if they had spoken to members of the NAACP since the two statements appeared, five said yes.

But only one—the one quoted above—said that he felt apologetic toward the NAACP.

Had they *personally* experienced any discrimination at the university? Seven answered "yes," seven "no" and one said "it is difficult to answer." Those who answered "yes" said "from other students," and also said "from other athletes and the physical education faculty." Specifically they endured: name calling, warnings by coaches not to become "involved" with white girls, receiving lower grades in physical education classes than they felt they deserved, and hearing teachers tell "Uncle Tom" jokes.

When asked: "If you had the chance to do it over, which university would you most like to attend?" eight chose the University of Illinois. Of those choosing other schools, five gave as reasons: "a more liberal racial climate," or "you can go places with a white girl without being disliked or looked at too hard."

In summary: The NAACP attacked the Athletic Association because they felt they had evidence of a continuing pattern of racial discrimination within the coaching staff, and that they could convince the university administration of it only if they galvanized public sentiment. A strong majority of the Negro athletes, organized and led by one of their colleagues, resented the NAACP's intrusion into their affairs, particularly without consultation, advice, or consent.

But a number of vexing and significant questions still remain: Was the case against the university and the Athletic Association strong enough to stand up in a formal public hearing? Why did the Negro athletes seem, relatively, to be so cool to civil rights issues? Why *didn't* the NAACP discuss the matter with some of the Negro athletes before acting?

To take the case to the public without securing the support of the athletes was politically foolish—in Lenin's terms, it was "political adventurism"—leading a revolution with no following. But this action did not cause the rupture between the NAACP and the athletes—rather it was a manifestation of other disorders, and a symptom of the social distance that separates Negroes from their leadership. We believe that this gulf is, most regrettably, grounded in the stigma of intellectual inferiority.

The cliche that beefy athletes recruited to play in highly commercialized college sports, especially football, whether Negro Americans from the slums or white Americans from the mines and fields, are stupid, lower class, and uncouth is certainly not new and not based on race. Athletes, white and black, are frequently referred to by other students as "animals." But the white student does not feel that the behavior of white athletes reflects on him; while the tenuous intellectual identity of Negroes makes them fear being classified with Negro athletes, and resaddled with this stigma.

But the stigma of inferiority also infected the Negro athletes, whether it seemed to come from the whites or their own people, and whether it was addressed to them as Negroes or as athletes.

But while this resentment may explain the rupture between the two groups, we are still left with the fundamental indifference of the Negro athletes here (and perhaps in general) to civil rights. Most athletes agree, it seems to us, that they had suffered discrimination from coaches and fellow students. Most believe that the Athletic Association and the Department of Physical Education give them lower grades than they deserve, prevent them from gaining recognition in certain sports, and police their social activities.

But in spite of these facts, Negro athletes, if they had not been organized, would have stayed out of the conflict.

Why—especially if, in fact, many of the athletes believe in the truth of the NAACP charges? We do not accept the argument that they were coerced by threats from the university that they would lose their athletic scholarships (many of them were graduating seniors) or in other ways suffer if they did not announce their disapproval.

We think that the most reasonable explanation lies in the image that the athletes have of themselves, and in their goals. Unlike many of the other Negro students on the campus they do not come from middle class families; almost all of them are from lower class families, from Southern rural areas or big city Northern slums. They are college students and not common laborers or high school dropouts because they are athletes. Their hopes for the future are tied to success in collegiate and professional sports—an industry dominated by whites. As individuals, many may resent strongly the discrimination they perceive all too clearly, but they see little to be gained by joining an organization which might protect them from verbal barbs, but hurt their chances of success in the one area in which they are skilled.

Success in athletics depends on individual achievement and recognition by the coaches and managers of the sport. The crucial figures in the lives of the athletes are the coaches and trainers who work with them. If they are to permanently escape from their backgrounds, they must have support. The NAACP and other civil rights organizations cannot write their ticket for social and financial success. So they identify with, they spend their time with, and they attach their hopes to the world of sports and to people who can train and grant them recognition in that world.

Further, we received the continuous impression—though it was only an impression—that an athlete senses discrimination to the degree he is unsuccessful in athletics. If he is doing well he is not likely to feel any discrimination. Moreover, he is likely to be happy with the university. But if he is doing badly in athletics, feelings of antagonism and insecurity are likely to be expressed as feelings that he is being discriminated against both by the coaching staff and by teachers and students. (In a separate study, a student in one of the author's classes interviewed some of the white athletes. He reported that many of them believe that the Negro players receive preferential consideration from the coaches and teaching staff, and "get all the breaks.")

Finally, the alleged discrimination within the Athletic Association was an issue seized upon to express symbolically an ineffable and inchoate feeling of mistreatment. There was much more than a case of discrimination at issue here. The attack on the Athletic Association expressed a real grievance, albeit not the grievance specifically charged. The Athletic Association served as a symbol which coalesced and expressed the Negroes' general alienation from and unhappiness with the university. The NAACP was not out in this case to save the athletes from themselves or the Athletic Association, but to galvanize public sentiment behind the general plight of the Negro at the University of Illinois and not the specific plight of an athlete warned about dating white girls.

The move backfired. First, because the Negro athletes did not share the same sense of alienation—they were better integrated into the structure of the university because of their involvement in athletics, and especially because they knew that success in sports, and not other Negroes, would determine their futures. Second, because the administration was too near-sighted to be able to distinguish between a demand for sympathy and understanding for the Negro student with a demand for the resolution of a particular case.

The NAACP never asked for a judicial hearing in which

to present charges. In all probability, they could not have presented a clear case. But even more than that, perhaps, they did not want a judicial victory. What they wanted was proof that the university understood the problems of Negro students, and was on their side—but they did not get it.

November 1966

Dynamic Young Fogies...
Rebels on the Right

LAWRENCE F. SCHIFF

From the bearded poet to the motorcycle delinquent, American adolescents usually go through a period of uncertainty and search, of trying to break away from old controls and standards, and of trying to establish their own identities and personalities.

As psychiatrist Erik H. Erikson puts it, youth searches for "fidelity"—"something and somebody to be true to"—and "often tests extremes before settling on a considered course." This period in adolescence often involves the rejection of things as they are, or as society says they should be.

So it seems an amazing paradox that many young people today, in a small but apparently growing movement, have dedicated themselves to promoting *greater* conservatism, *more* tradition, and *more* devotion and adherence to the values not only of an older generation, but apparently even of an older century.

The conservative movement began in 1960 on the wave of enthusiasm generated by the abortive attempt to get the vice-presidential nomination for Barry Goldwater. The excitement, the spontaneous appearance of so many young conservatives, led to the formation of the Young Americans for Freedom—or YAF. Since then, fed by the rise of other non-affiliated but similarly oriented local college groups, the campus conservative movement has become a fairly successful and going concern. There is no doubt that, paradoxical or not, a small but sizable segment of our young people have found something in this movement to which they respond, and that seems to meet their internal and external demands.

In my study I found that about two-thirds of those interviewed had undergone such a strong change in belief and behavior in coming to conservatism that it could properly be said that they had experienced a form of "conversion." (The other third had simply followed comfortably along the right-wing paths already set by their parents.) These converts, I discovered, had gone through crises and events that were very revealing about their development as adolescents and their total development as human beings.

Specifically, I have found that at the various stages of adolescence different kinds of persons were attracted by conservatism, for different reasons, and in response to different needs. It matters a great deal whether the conversion occurred *immediately following puberty* (between 12 and 17), or in *late adolescence* (beyond 17). There is some overlap; but the two groups are distinctive, each with its own dynamics and style.

The late converts—whom I call "the obedient rebels"— were the ones most representative of campus conservative activists. Typically they were from homes very much concerned with high status and achievement. In almost all cases their early experiences were dominated by a determined parent, or parents, with detailed and ambitious expectations for their children. All but one were eldest or only sons and the burden of parental ambition fell on them. The obedient rebels (at least in the early years and again after conversion) were usually considered the "good boys" of their families.

Each "rebelled"—sometimes because he felt he could not live up to or realize himself under such pressure—or departed to some degree from the path set out for him. But the revolt was not without peril. Suddenly he would be horrified to discover (on the campus, in the armed services, or among the lower-classes) that he was surrounded by "radicalism," "immorality," or personal hardship— something for which his comfortable background had not prepared him. He would reject the new environment totally and become converted to a conservatism not much different from the one he had left in the first place—but which, superficially at least, he had accepted on his own initiative and conviction.

Psychologically, in essence, his conversion was a reaction to the threat of genuine personality change—which allows great creative possibilities, but also involves dangers. In effect he had come to the pit of change, looked down into it, and turned back, rejecting all alternatives beyond the reaffirmation of obedience; if the non-convert conservatives had never left home, the obedient rebels had returned home.

The *early* adolescent converts, however, exhibited a strikingly different and even more interesting pattern—one signifying a very different way of coping with adolescence. Their conversions were made during, and as part of, the turbulent and formative center of adolescence, and were intertwined, warp and woof, with the demands, potentialities, problems, and limits of that period. The personality changes were reflected in the conversion experience itself.

Where the obedient rebel came to conversion as a result of shock and repulsion (a negative reaction), the early convert came as a result of attraction, or recognition, because he saw something that seemed to meet his needs (for positive reasons). The late convert came to escape from and to deny real change; the early convert came seeking answers and seeking change. His conversion was change itself.

The late convert identified with the overall posture and prestige of the new conservatism, rather than with its detailed content. He was concerned mostly with status, with position, with social identification, with respectability and role—not with passionate belief. As such he could accept its doctrine totally, without much quibble, since what counted was what it stood for, rather than what it was. But the early convert's acceptance of conservatism was specific, personal, immediate, discriminating, and emotional; and he was much more interested in content, as he understood it, than in form.

To understand the contrasts between early and late conversion it is best to go back to the beginnings, in boyhood, and follow the process through time.

As noted, the late converts typically came from families with great determination to see that their children rose in the world. They were under great pressure to achieve and conform—as the interviews revealed.

—Herron's father, a highly successful independent lawyer, early and ardently began to infuse his young son with the spirit of his "adherence to strict moral standards" . . .

—Finestock's immigrant father received a primary school education here and then in true Horatio Alger fashion, rose . . . to put together a fabulously successful business. He intended that his son would actualize his success. . . .

Under such pressure they bent; each in his own way,

always covertly and at times involuntarily, they veered from the too high and too rigid parental blueprint.

—Herron . . . chafing under . . . his father's tutelage, began to channel his energies into activities only marginally related to the development of intellect or character. . . . Throughout his adolescence he managed to balance off his resentment against his father by avoiding overt disobedience, always maintaining the form but not the substance of his father's preachments.

—Finestock's father had "pulled strings" to get him into a first-rate college, but after two unhappy years there he flunked out.

Their conversions, when they came, were a reaction to the new standards to which their rebellion had exposed them. They rejected this new environment totally—and as individuals, rather than as a result of being solicited by other conservatives. While it may have set them apart for a time from most of their immediate fellows it did give them a reassuring image and identity, and it led them back toward their parents.

—Herron's conversion took place while he was stationed abroad in the Navy. Disturbed by the "slothfulness" and "self-indulgent habits" of the local citizenry, he had a sudden realization of "the consequences of not subscribing to a strict moral code."

—Manning reacted to his college's total climate. He found himself "appalled and amazed" about some of the college newspaper editorials . . . "disappointed" with the college's moral climate. . . .

Conversion for the early adolescents presents a striking contrast. They did not turn from what they found in adolescence to go back to a childhood pattern. In fact, just the opposite—their adolescent conversions were a rejection of their beginnings.

Typically, the early convert came from a family where relationships were intense, and often stressful, unsettling, or full of strife:

—For O'Hara, childhood was . . . far from tranquil. His father (was) a man with a "quick temper" and "quick to criticize" . . . there were always "big arguments." "At one time I looked upon him as the oppressor of both me and my mother, and now I look on them both as in the same boat."

—Mann recalls himself as "a rather uncontrolled" kid, "disciplined from above. But inside I was rebellious . . . I was probably a pretty wretched kid."

—Arnold relates a persistent "inferiority complex. . . . I didn't conform to my mother's beliefs. . . . She kept repeating how no-good I was and how she wished I'd never been born. (This) had quite a dire effect on me."

Two of the young converts had alcoholic fathers; two others came from homes in which chronic instability kept things "wound up and involved."

In all of these cases, the child's emotional life was hyperactive and somewhat uncontrolled. Unlike the late converts, childhood experiences stimulated, rather than molded, character. They would not, or could not, silently conform. These early converts entered adolescence with still smoldering, unsettled infantile residues that had to be worked out some way.

Not surprisingly therefore, virtually all experienced during adolescence a sharp break with the past.

O'Hara: "I was flamboyant originally and a social guy, and then all of a sudden, snap! After sophomore year (high school) I became an introvent, a searcher. . . . I realized I didn't want to be anything like my father was —not his profession, not his personality—and that's just what I was going to be. . . . I wanted to go out on my own—I couldn't stand my dad."

Others went through a social dislocation that served as the break between childhood and what followed:

—Howard, after years of wandering . . . with his Army doctor father . . . at the onset of high school . . . settled into . . . an upper-middle-class suburban community where the family's style of living rose sharply. (He) felt "a little out of place for the first couple of years" . . . in "a rebellion against the accepted ideas I found around me."

—Mann was cut off from his Jewish past in New York City when he became a congressional page. . . . Assigned to the Republican side of the House, he became thoroughly involved in "contacts with those with another point of view."

Three boys came from working-class homes. They broke away from parental patterns and chose their own college-bound paths early—and alone. No brothers or sisters followed.

My mother wasn't even sure I should go to college. I just told her I was going.

Parental values—and even parental models—become irrelevant as each pursued his own road to self-realization.

Our society, with its lack of ritualized organization, does not make the path of growth easy for the young. Peter Blos (*On Adolescence,* The Free Press, 1962) points out: "Where tradition and custom offer no unchallenged influence over the individual, the adolescent has to achieve by personal resourcefulness the adaptation that institutionalization does not offer him. On the other hand, this lack of institutionalized pattern opens up the opportunity for individual development, for the creation of a unique, highly original, and personal variation on tradition."

Thus, finally, this breakaway, whatever handicaps it imposed, also allowed the early converts to work out their own highly individual fates without the inhibitions of family control or tradition. And their conversions played key roles in this working-out.

For some, separation from their families began with the pain of severe withdrawal—"a self-inflicted purgatory."

—O'Hara: "I don't remember those years—I try to forget—don't think about it that much." Through his second year in high school he alternated between the "good works" of a Catholic social action group and quasi-delinquency, then suddenly "realized that there was hypocrisy in my life" and literally "pulled out . . ." spending much of the next two years trying to "settle it by lying down and thinking about myself."

—For Griffith the marriage of his sister (who had served as a mother substitute) brought on a depressive state for several years. . . . Through high school he was "introverted, very, very quiet. . . . (the kids') middle-class outlooks repulsed me. . . ."

—For Arnold and Wilson the challenge of adjustment proved unmanageable and led to . . . enlistment in the armed forces. . . .

For other converts the transition was more benign, but just as decisive.

From this "purgatory," this searching, they found and embraced conservatism.

—(Griffith's) exposure to and developing enthusiasm about the writings of Ayn Rand and Goldwater conservatism crystallized soon after . . . the death of his father and a year of emotional turmoil for his widowed mother.

—O'Hara: "I wanted to spread out. I almost became a priest; but it's a much greater task to do it on your own. That's what I'm working on now." During two summers . . . away from home he made his first contacts with conservatism. "Things were so completely different . . . just remade me—my dad wasn't around—I made friends fast —everything else was forgotten."

For working-class converts the conversion came when they had replaced their family ties with outside middle-class and conservative models.

In sum, these early conversions came about because they served to meet and answer the challenges of adolescence for these young men. They fit Blos's contention that: "Adolescence, not only in spite of, but rather because of, its emotional turmoil, often affords spontaneous recovery from debilitating childhood influences. . . ." and Erikson's suggestion that: "We look at adolescence not as an affliction, but as a normal phase of increased conflict characterized by a high growth potential."

Typically, the early convert had a "hero," who had great influence, both as recruiter and example.

There was a counselor there, a man who appealed to me. It turned out he had a ranch in Arizona, he was born on it and he was a conservative . . . that's where I first became interested . . . he was a cool guy and he seemed reasonable. . . . Naturally this transferred into the policies he put forth.

William F. Buckley, the popular and vocal editor of the *National Review,* is a key hero:

Well, my romance with him—first of all I think he has tremendous style—secondly he's a more complete man . . . he doesn't hedge—he says it, he's not afraid to say it. Lord, that is a tremendous quality in this age.

The archetypal heroes for the early convert, of course, are those that Ayn Rand creates—and Miss Rand herself. She, too, is "not afraid to say it." Her creations are heroic in the fullest and most uninhibited sense of the word. Existing outside of time, history, and social circumstance, they are unfettered men, free of any social or personal responsibilities or knowledge that might slow down their single-minded pursuit of their self-interest (which, as it happens, is also the greatest public good, since they are a unique breed of supermen whose genius is all that keeps the world moving). Miss Rand's unabashed "philosophy" is outside the conservative mainstream. It is avowedly atheistic and egotistical and is meant to shock the conventional, so it is taboo to the obedient rebels. But how many teen-agers, smarting under parental, social, and school controls which they find false and binding, would not thrill to the story of an architect who refused to compromise with his paying clients and blew up a building development because someone tampered with his design?

Unlike the "lone wolf" obedient rebel, the early convert is usually converted *by* somebody or *with* somebody—it is a social process. He becomes part of a group of similar persons who give support both to him and his belief. Conservatism is woven into the fabric of his relationships:

—Madding "got hold of the (John Birch) *Blue Book* and passed it on to my friends; nearly all were very much impressed. . . ."

—Riley joined his campus YAF chapter because "I liked the people in it."

The early adolescent undergoes a deep conversion. His whole "self-system" is involved. His personality and emotions have been expressed in the act, not just his public face.

—O'Hara (had) an experience of intense self examination which lasted through several "extremely turbulent years, psychologically and emotionally." He now sees conservatism as the only philosophy "congruent with my whole philosophy of life." For O'Hara to arrive at this point required a "personal experience of God" . . . "Inspiration first and examination later."

—Griffith found himself adopting political ideas that

were the opposite of his father's. "I suppose there's some deep psychological basis."

—Mann's response to a suggestion of his mother that he would have to become a Democrat in order to be elected. . . . "She doesn't understand that this would mean changing me as a person."

Commitment among adolescents tends to be "all out." Among the conservatives this takes the form of "gung-ho" anti-communism (a strange use of the old Chinese Communist slogan). With the older converts this was often directed most harshly at what they suspected were anti-anti-Communists in their midst—the enemy within—which may, psychologically, be an overt rejection of forbidden internal impulses. The early converts on the other hand seemed to have no such internal conflicts. The enemy was outside their ranks—distinct, identifiable, and real. "Gung-ho" meant to them what it did to Carlson's Raiders.

Conversion did, however, in other ways shed revealing lights on their deep inner needs and impulse life:

People are afraid of nuclear weapons (but) I don't fear the bomb . . . in a way I think it'd be an interesting experience . . . (I) would've enjoyed being a part of the Korean War. . . . I would've enjoyed shooting a few of those guys—they're our enemies.

The process of differentiating the self from the surrounding environment, a crucial part of self-realization, received dramatic form among the early converts. As Edgar Friedenberg describes it: "The oppositional, rebellious, and restive strivings, the stages of experimentation, the testing of the self by going to excess—all these have a positive usefulness . . . for self-definition." For several the conversion was a part of the means through which these strivings were expressed:

—Mann, aware of the unpopularity of his views, particularly back home, reacted with "a kind of strange and exaltative joy that someone was finding what I was say-ing especially incomprehensible."

—Griffith: "It's 'in' to be liberal. . . . Every once in a while, sitting at a table, everybody nods in agreement—and it's a little bit difficult to dissent. That's a very nice word, 'dissent,' and I think it should be preserved."

—Howard's original conservative thinking was formu-lated as a part of "a rebellion against the accepted ideas I found around me." He became, "by way of argument," a proponent of Herbert Hoover.

—O'Hara enjoys thinking of himself . . . as someone . . . able to "throw everything out."

Note the ease—indeed the relish and pride—in accepting the image of the self as iconoclast. They often seemed equally as concerned with what was "not me" within the spectrum of conservatism (a concern significantly different from that of the obedient rebels, who repudiated dissen-sion within the ranks). What is distinctive is the emphasis on defining the self as in conflict with and yet as part of surrounding influences.

These young men are, more than most, "tuned in" on themselves—they have a heightened awareness of them-selves.

—O'Hara reports feeling "as a man alone" after he "jumped out on my own, suddenly."

—Mann . . . thinks "everyone is basically insular . . . I am . . . everyone is distinct from everyone else deep inside. . . . There are many times when the most precious thing to me is to just sit down and think my own thoughts."

Important in this process of self-realization is the early convert's emphasis on the he-man self-image of conserva-tism—the rugged individualist, the combat soldier, Ayn Rand's hypermasculine heroes—an identification that might serve also to still any secret doubts about his own masculinity.

The early convert is at this stage still an unstable and incomplete human being—disengaged and aggrandized—a volatile configuration of conflicting strivings, tendencies, growth potentialities, and neurotic dangers. Since he is unfinished, only on rare occasions in the present sample did the political beliefs formed at conversion not undergo further important change.

Finally therefore, and most significantly, the early convert is engaged in a dynamic open-end process of alteration —similar, in this respect, to almost all other adolescents. He is on the "right track," but he is also traveling, and the end is neither in sight nor completely known. The obedient rebel has arrived; his beliefs and posture are round, firm, and fully packed. His conversion resulted in reduced tension and resolved conflict, and he will not again willingly risk uncertainty. Change is suspect and may be abhorrent. But to the early convert change is not at all unwelcome; he looks forward to it as another adventure. He delicately balances tentativeness and commitment:

I feel that every student is essentially an observer in that he need not be committed to too many things. I have definitely not committed to conservative politics. . . . I'll give you my tendency, not my opinion. Opinion implies commitment.

In many cases he shows himself flexible, open to outside influences:

Madding . . . is unsure if the economics course in which he is currently enrolled might not be "liberalizing me." . . . "Right now I'm just feeling my way along."

Actual changes take place:

Howard began as a Randian disciple and then . . . "found I was looking for some 'new departure' in politics in the individualist direction, something not a revolt or return to the past."

In short and in summary, early conversion for these boys was a part of continuing development. It contributed substantially to self-definition; it helped integrate the entire personality; it helped the adolescent toward positive sexual identity, and the ability to have close relationships with other people. The conversion of the typical obedient rebel restored and bound him to his original role. The overall effect of the conversion of the young adolescent was emancipation.

But it is apparently true even of the young converts that, compared to the non-conservatives, they feel a need for all-inclusive answers, spelled out. Our society, according to Erik Erikson, requires of its youth many contradictory things, necessitating, therefore, "a distaste for ideological explicitness." The young conservatives need more than that: as convert Mann put it, "you must have a point of view . . . a basic premise . . . or everything is senseless."

Against the anti-hero of the modern novel with his existential despair, the analytic critic who debunks old traditions, and the disillusioned old radicals from the depression, the far right throws the heroic novel, the embattled and engaged young critic, and the refurbished old radical who has found another New Jerusalem—this one on the road back to Adam Smith. The new convert may not understand all of this, but it does give him something with sharp edges on which to shape himself, something more than the simple necessity to "get along." In this strident ideology and movement, he can find an object able to take on his fantasies and fears, to allow extreme possibilities to be tested, to provide space to work out problems, and room to grow or to regress.

The young converts found in conservatism a way to

bring internal needs and fears into the open in the form of ideas and actions, there to communicate them, to shape them, to face them consciously and render them amenable to control. But the obedient rebels were more interested in restriction, in cutting off internal debate and conflict. It is paradoxical, therefore, but inevitable, that the obedient rebel demanded total and rigid conformity to conservative doctrine but was not emotionally involved in it very much; while the young converts cared passionately, but kept straying from orthodoxy.

Significantly then, the end for the young converts is not yet:

> O'Hara: "Where I go from here I don't know. Terms like 'truth' and 'right' and 'wrong' are fine . . . except in the sense that they've come to be pretty much meaningless. . . . But I think we can give them some meaning."

November 1966

FURTHER READING SUGGESTED BY THE AUTHOR:

They'd Rather Be Right, by Edward Cain. New York: Macmillan, 1963. Factual, useful study of the current rightwing youth movement.

Youth: Change and Challenge, edited by Erik Erikson (based on Daedalus, Vol. 91, 1962). Essays on current youth around the world.

The Vanishing Adolescent, by Edgar Z. Friedenberg. Boston, Mass.: Beacon Press, 1959. Social criticism of American society's effect on adolescents, particularly the high school.

Ending
Campus Drug Incidents

HOWARD S. BECKER

The use of drugs—primarily marijuana and LSD—has become an increasingly important and time-consuming problem on college campuses. Much of the thinking and writing (that done by adults, anyway) focuses on the drug use itself, asking why so many students take drugs and what can be done to prevent them, or lessen the impact of their use of drugs.

But instead of asking why students use drugs, let us ask how a campus comes to have a drug incident—thus suggesting that we *ought* to be concerned with a problem somewhat different from the one we conventionally are.

I propose this, first, because it is very likely impossible, given our resources and our will, to stop students from using drugs. No college administration has the personnel to root out drug use by itself. (It may try, however, to achieve the same end by opening the college to undercover agents of off-campus police forces, or it may—as in the recent action at Stony Brook, Long Island—find off-campus forces invading the campus openly, without asking permission first.)

In addition, we need more knowledge before we can get any firm answer to the question of why students use drugs —and any program designed to eradicate drug use not founded on this knowledge will surely fail. Third, it seems to me that the processes involved in a campus drug incident do not require intensive study, and that we may find a way out of our current difficulties by attacking the problem at this level.

Finally, available evidence and the experience of campus physicians indicate that drugs are a minor health hazard. LSD apparently presents some difficulties, but marijuana (the most widely-used psychedelic) has no demonstrable bad effects. Campus psychiatrists know that alcohol presents them with far worse problems. In short, students who think there is no good reason for attempting to restrict student drug use are right.

I thus mean to distinguish campus drug incidents from campus drug use. Students may use drugs without incidents occurring. An incident occurs when students use drugs, the college administration is confronted with the fact publicly, and it takes some punitive action in consequence. The press, radio, and TV are frequently involved.

What do students and administrators do that produces the typical campus incident? Students contribute to the growing number of incidents in two ways. First, more and more of them use drugs. My guess is that marijuana use is now viewed by many college students in the same way that chastity is said to be viewed by college women. Once students did not recognize any legitimate argument in favor of drug use; they knew that it was, quite simply, "wrong," just as the "nice" college girls knew that "nice girls don't." But college girls now see chastity as a matter for individual decision; they can envision many circumstances in which premarital intercourse is morally acceptable. So each girl must make up her mind for herself; she no longer believes that an absolute moral rule governs such decisions. Similarly with drugs. Students who once thought all drug use immoral now believe that the consequences of use are so negligible that it is a matter for each student to decide.

Further, the greater availability of scientific information convinces students, approaching it as they do in a rational and "scientific" manner, that they have nothing to fear. This, of course, occurs most frequently with respect to marijuana, where the scientific evidence most clearly favors that interpretation.

But increased student drug use alone is not sufficient to create a campus drug incident. For that to happen, students must also be caught, which is happening more and more frequently. Students get caught in a variety of ways. A number of incidents have been triggered by students who sold marijuana to policemen. Sometimes students smoke the drug so openly as to make detection almost inevitable —the very openness of the act, in fact, makes the police or other officials feel that they are being taunted and thus increases the students' chances of arrest. Sometimes students create a campus incident by giving drugs to other people without their knowledge, possibly as a prank. These people may respond very badly, and official action is provoked by the medical opinion that drug use is thus very dangerous.

What students do to provoke a drug incident, then, is to get caught. And they get caught for two reasons: ignorance and ideology. They are either ignorant of the devices and precautions that might protect them against arrest, or they are willing to risk it on ideological grounds.

Most of the college students who use drugs today have no desire to get caught. On the contrary, they fear arrest and its effect on their lives. They do not want to be kicked out of school, or have police records, or be branded as dope fiends. But they have learned to use drugs in an atmosphere where strict security measures do not seem essential to avoid arrest, and where no one has told them what those measures are.

Drug users of past generations knew that they had to fear the police. These experienced users were cautious about whom they bought drugs from and whom they sold them to, about where they used drugs and whom they allowed to know, about where they kept their supplies and about the people before whom they would dare to appear "high." These precautions were part of the culture that drug users learned at the same time they learned to use drugs, and the necessity for such precautions and their character were passed on from one user to another. It appears now that a large number of college students have gained access to drugs without acquiring this aspect of the drug-using culture. They know how to get high, but they don't know how to get high without getting caught.

Other students, a smaller number, get caught for ideological reasons. Some believe they have a constitutional right to get high on drugs. (Indeed, constitutional issues have been raised in many cases, some of which will probably find their way to the Supreme Court: These students may be right.) They want to use drugs, feel that they are legally entitled to do so, and wish to provoke a legal confrontation on the question. Or they simply do not wish to bother about being secretive. They may adopt an ideology of psychological freedom, believing that the psychic energy they expend in secretive maneuvers could be spent better in other ways. They recognize that they are taking a chance, but consider the chance worth the price. Either of these ideologies leads students to be quite open about their drug use, perhaps using drugs in public places, or announcing publicly that they use drugs.

In short, whether out of ideology or ignorance, students use drugs with increasing openness and lack of caution. This leads to situations in which they are very likely to get caught and become the objects of publicity. And at this point college administrations complete the process of creating a campus drug incident.

College administrations, as a rule, respond to the pressures of publicity by taking some kind of action. They will very likely not have a reasoned approach to the problem. Confronted with letters and calls from angry and worried parents, with strong pressure from boards of trustees (and, in the case of public institutions, from state legislatures), with continuing newspaper questioning, they act hastily. They may expel the student. They may pass new harsh regulations, or make new interpretations of the broad discretionary powers they already have.

These responses assume that the number of drug users is small; that, once weeded out, they will not be replaced by new users; and that the problem can be dealt with within the confines of the campus proper. But none of these assumptions is correct. The number of users is large and growing; they cannot be weeded out, only driven underground. Since students can always purchase drugs "in town," in nearby cities, or on other campuses, no college can contain the activity on its own. So harsh action by university authorities simply brings even more cases to light and increases the unfavorable publicity—at least until students get the message and become more cautious.

The same considerations apply to the increased surveillance

that students are subjected to. Many of the actions students are now caught for might have gone unnoticed, flagrant as they are, if campus officials had not alerted campus police, dormitory counselors, student-health personnel, and others to bring relevant evidence to the attention of the authorities. Some of this increased attention followed F.D.A. Commissioner James L. Goddard's appeal for such cooperation with federal and local law-enforcement officials; some was probably a simple response to massive national publicity. All increases in surveillance, of course, multiply the number of cases that come to public attention as campus drug incidents and thus increase the difficulties the surveillance was supposed to solve.

Administrators take strong actions because they fear there may be some danger to the students involved—and because of the pressure of publicity.

Many deans of students worry about the dangers of drug use. After all, we cannot expect that they will have expert knowledge of drugs. Nor is the most appropriate time for such an educational effort likely to be in the midst of a great public-relations crisis.

In any case, knowledge alone will not solve the problem. Many college administrators know perfectly well that marijuana is a harmless drug. Nevertheless, their public-relations problem persists. We can see how the maintenance of a favorable image lies at the heart of the administrators' concern by comparing the amount of activity against marijuana and LSD use to that against the use of amphetamines, quite widespread on many campuses for years (students use Benzedrine as an aid for staying up and studying at exam time). I do not recall any administration's taking severe action on the use of amphetamines, though I believe that physicians agree that amphetamines are potentially a great deal more dangerous than marijuana. And we can note the same kind of differential response to students' use of alcohol.

Suppose we take as our goal the reduction of the number of campus drug incidents. This might be accomplished by trying to do away with student drug use. But students want to use drugs and can easily do so; few college administrations will decide to use the totalitarian methods that would be required. One might institute a daily search of all student rooms and perhaps, in addition, inaugurate a campus "stop-and-frisk" law. But they are not going to do these things, so student drug use will continue.

We might also educate administrators to take a calmer view of the problem. This, no doubt, would do some good, but even the most knowledgeable administration would not be able to avoid the difficulties of a public-relations crisis.

We might, finally, educate students to take precautions to avoid detection. If an educational program of this kind, perhaps sponsored by the student government, were started on a campus, and if students took their lesson seriously, many fewer might engage in those actions likely to provoke arrest or detection. There would be fewer incidents to make publicity about, fewer incidents for the administration to respond to. The administration no doubt would still be aware that students were using drugs on campus, but it would not be confronted publicly with that use and would not be required to respond.

If students could be so educated, some kind of implicit bargain might be struck between university administrators and student drug users, a bargain not unlike the one that seems to characterize homosexuality on most college campuses. All campuses of any size have a homosexual underground that probably includes both students and faculty members, yet we hear very little about homosexual incidents on campus. Administrations seldom seem to get upset about this problem, seldom take strong punitive measures, and almost never make a big public outcry about it. I suspect that this is because they have, in effect, come to terms with the homosexual community on their campus. They regard it as an evil, no doubt, but not as an evil that can be easily done away with. They worry about the physical and psychological harm the community's existence may cause members and nonmembers. But they know they must live with it, and they do. They take action only when some provocative incident occurs, such as when a student blackmails a faculty members, when minors are involved, or when the matter comes to police attention (as it seldom does). In effect, the homosexual community and the university administration have made a bargain that goes something like this: The homosexuals agree to keep things out of the newspapers and the administration agrees not to look for trouble. An ethic of "live and let live" prevails.

This strikes me as the most likely solution to the problem of campus drug use. Administrators must take a calmer view of drug use, and students must become more cautious. The main obstacles to such a bargain will be nervous administrators afraid to take such a step, and ideological students who wish a confrontation on the issue.

But college administrators have learned to live with sex and drink. They may yet be able to learn to live with drugs as well.

April 1968

Not surprisingly, these modest suggestions provoked a variety of critical letters.

Howard Becker's solution to the student drug problem—that students be taught to use drugs covertly—reminds me of an argument I once heard for Murder, Inc. If you want someone killed, hire a stranger to do it. Then the act will seem irrational rather than motivated, and fewer people will worry about it. Or, better still, make murder legal; then, rest assured, the murder rate will drop dramatically.

Becker's argument is empty. In the first place, there is very clear evidence that most of the "mind-expanding" drugs either do definite damage to the brain, or cause people to do things that are injurious to others, things they probably would not ordinarily do. The statement, "Many college administrators know perfectly well that marihuana is a harmless drug," is based on flimsy factual data. Some 20 years ago a group of physicians in New York wrote a report, based largely on clinical, not experimental, studies, which concluded that the stuff was harmless. There has been next to no research since then; in point of fact, the methods used in that "research" paper (the "La Guardia Report") are so full of holes I have sometimes assigned students to read it as a good example of what to avoid when doing research.

It is quite true that alcohol is injurious; but it has been around a long time, and we know pretty well what it will do to you, and an elaborate social ritual has grown up around it to curtail its use and prevent people from using it beyond certain limits. No one is really sure just what marihuana, LSD, and so forth, do to people, and there is no way of setting limits. Until further research on animals and humans is forthcoming, therefore, I unhesitatingly endorse total and complete abstinence from these kinds of drugs as the only safe course for any sane person.

Which brings up an interesting point: Why take the stuff in the first place? Why the necessity for the underground? The few drug addicts I have tested, and the larger number whose records I have seen, all wish to escape reality, to return to an emotional level about that of a 3-year-old child (indeed, some are stuck at that level, and use the drug to stay there). My question is, why do we have a nation of teenage infants? And, for that matter, professors of sociology?

Stanley A. Rudin, Chief, Behavioral Research Laboratory
Rollman Psychiatric Institute, Cincinnati, Ohio

We feel that some comment on Becker's ingenious solution to drug problems is called for. Educating students in deviousness, and asking administrators to ignore the problem in hopes that it would somehow go away, are solutions of such originality that we are sure we should all respond by saying, "Now, why didn't I think of that!" Regardless of the degree of sophistication of this "new approach," we seriously question the accuracy of Becker's global "scientific" assertions about the harmlessness of marihuana.

We should tend to agree with Becker's implicit assumption that the laws relating to the use of marihuana leave a great deal to be desired. However, Becker implies that the only danger in marihuana use is a legal one. He states that "available evidence and the experience of campus physicians indicate drugs are a minor health hazard, . . . marihuana has no demonstrable bad effects." This is so contrary to our own experience as campus psychiatrists that we must question whether Becker is at all aware of the "available evidence and the experience of campus physicians."

At the University of North Carolina Student Health Service, we have seen a significant number of individuals who have had serious and often disabling accentuation of existing problems because of their use of marihuana. To a lesser extent, we have also seen individuals who have had serious psychiatric difficulties precipitated by the use of marihuana. (See Keeler, "Adverse Reactions to Marihuana," *American Journal of Psychiatry,* November, 1967.)

Surveys conducted in areas where marihuana is prevalent, and the relatively few experimental studies of the drug, have indicated a fair frequency of adverse reactions. These studies, however, have been questioned on several bases. Probably the most critical is that a predisposition to difficulty must have existed in the user for trouble to occur. However, unless one takes the monolithic approach that a drug that does not produce psychopathology in everyone is utterly safe, this does not serve to exonerate marihuana.

The allegation (repeated several times in the article and apparently the basis for his entire argument) that use of marihuana is completely harmless is *not* supported by available evidence. The risks in terms of the frequency of adverse reactions may be small, but may be of sufficiently serious nature that some individuals may elect not to run such a risk, particularly if the potential benefits are also small. For the individual who does have a serious, incapacitating reaction related to marihuana use, the problem is no longer "a minor health hazard." It is little solace to him or to the physician responsible for his treatment that some individuals also react adversely to alcohol or, for that matter, to penicillin. The comparisons to potential dangers of other drugs (amphetamines and alcohol) that Becker makes not only beg the question, but are a retreat to authority, personal opinion, and argument by analogy. In addition, he falsely ascribes to medical authority a lot more unanimity and a lot more certainty than is justified by the small amount of available evidence. His cavalier contribution toward understanding and dealing with a complex medical and sociological problem is scientifically irresponsible to a degree incompatible with Becker's esteemed scholarly position and reputation.

We're afraid our agreement with Becker's article is limited to the proposition that education is important: Education about the possible effects of marihuana is of great importance for students who may use it, for administrators who may react to it, and for sociologists who may write about it.

Clifford B. Reifler, M.D., assistant professor of psychiatry and senior psychologist to the Health Service
Martin H. Keeler, M.D., associate professor of psychiatry
The University of North Carolina, Chapel Hill, N. C.

. . . there is far from unanimous support by informed people of Becker's statement that marihuana is nonaddictive. It does tend to be psychically addictive, and this kind of addiction is the worst. But even apart from this, marihuana use tends to lead to the dangerous and highly addictive heroin, because the users want something with a stronger kick.

To the extent that Becker's article may influence the thinking of young people and of those responsible for their welfare, it will have extremely unhappy social effects.

Dwight E. Allen
Bradenton, Fla.

Howard Becker's advice regarding the campus drug-use problem is refreshing in its practicality and realism. Certainly it is the *incidents* involving marihuana use that are a problem, and their reduction in frequency—not only on campuses but elsewhere—would be a boon to all concerned. I wish more professors had the courage to publicly declaim the impracticality of rooting out the growing use of marihuana.

There are some flaws, however, in Becker's position. First, the use of drugs is probably growing as fast among faculty as among students. The article treats drug use entirely as a student problem. Are we to believe that graduate students who blow grass suddenly stop when they get their Ph.D.s and join the faculty?

Second, Becker concedes that marihuana use is not intrinsically wrong. The wrongness comes from rocking the academic boat by getting caught. The decision to smoke marihuana, like the decision regarding chastity or homosexuality, "is a decision for each student to decide." (I would add, for each faculty member as well.) If this is true, then there is an important and unavoidable issue. Why should public policy toward essentially harmless personal behavior, as expressed in law and consequent police harassment, be allowed to continue? Why do all of us, through our political structures, go on making decisions for other people—decisions that are inherently personal? These issues need to be confronted and the students willing to confront them should be applauded. Yet Becker admonishes them not to cause "public-relations crises" for administrators.

Brooks K. Truitt, Social Service Administrator
Department of Social Welfare, Los Angeles, Calif.

I replied to the letters as follows:

In response to the letters about my recommendations for ending campus drug incidents, I should like to comment on three points:

Some of the writers believe that marihuana is more than a "minor health hazard." In part, these complaints illustrate the double standard of evidence often used in defending existing laws: Marihuana is condemned by standards that would also require us to ban alcohol, while alcohol is excused on grounds that would also excuse marihuana. More important, these complaints fail to distinguish medical from political judgments. I did not intend to suggest that marihuana is perfectly safe; nothing in the world is. But does it cause adverse reactions (that is the medical judgment) in sufficient numbers and of sufficient severity to warrant official intervention (that is the political judgment)? The question is not whether the individual elects to run risks but whether the public interest justifies the state's refusing to allow him to do so. That is why the common comparisons with alcohol and tobacco, far from begging the question, are very much to the point. They show that our national policy is generally to allow people to do themselves a good deal of damage, much more than marihuana has ever been demonstrated to cause.

Some of the writers seem appalled by the notion of a university administration accepting drug use and learning to live with it. But I don't know what other sensible course there is when the practice itself cannot be stopped. To suggest that administrators can get rid of drug use altogether is a pipe dream; they have, as I suggested originally, neither the will nor the resources. They do not get to choose between effective prohibition and cowardly acceptance. Their choice is between ineffective trouble-making and realistic coping. That may shock some people. But I don't suppose I need to tell psychiatrists that reality can sometimes be shocking. These critics would have had a stronger argument had they suggested *how* they were going to do away with drug use, so that it would *not* be necessary for college administrators to live with it.

It is refreshing to be attacked by Mr. Truitt from the left, but I think the attack is misplaced, for I agree completely that the present laws are unjust and unnecessary, and that no one should be punished under federal, state, or local law for taking such drugs. But I think, too, that those laws are not going to be changed easily or quickly and that, *in the meantime,* colleges will be confronted with "the drug problem" and find themselves in situations requiring action and a policy. My comment was addressed to that specific situation. I'm sorry if it seemed to imply an acceptance of the present laws, for I only meant to suggest how, under present arrangements, colleges could go about their educational business and students about their work and play without undue interference. We must all applaud the courage of those who attack unjust laws but, on the other hand, no one ought to become a test case by accident—and that is what happens to too many people now.

The Psychiatrist
As Double Agent

THOMAS SZASZ

"One of the casualties in the mass murder ... at the University of Texas was the confidential relationship between a troubled student, Charles Whitman, and the university psychiatrist, Dr. Maurice D. Heatly. Dr. Heatly released to a news conference the text of his report on Whitman's visit to him . . ., including intimate troubles of the Whitman family."—*The New York Times*

It is customary to cast discussions of college psychiatry into the framework of medicine and public health. This is consistent with the view that psychiatric services are a type of health care to be dispensed through the school's general health program. It is inconsistent, however, with the work the college psychiatrist actually does and is expected to do.

I have long maintained that the psychiatrist impersonates the medical role; actually, he is an interpreter of moral rules and an enforcer of social laws and expectations. This is especially true of the bureaucratic psychiatrist—that is, of the psychiatrist who is a paid agent of a social organization, rather than of an individual patient. If we wish to confront the true nature of mental health practices in colleges, then, we must remove psychiatry from its hiding place, the infirmary, where—housed with medical, dental, radiological, and surgical services—it is disguised as just another medical specialty. Only then will we be able to examine it as a moral and political enterprise.

I use the word "moral" to refer to the principles of conduct governing an individual or a group; and the word "politics" to refer to the relationship between rulers and the ruled. My present aim, then, is to examine the principles of conduct governing college psychiatrists and the relationships between these authorities and their subjects.

D. L. Farnsworth describes the activities of the college psychiatrist in his recent book, *Psychiatry, Education, and the Young Adult.* According to Farnsworth, himself a college psychiatrist, "Those who work in college psychiatric services do not consider it the duty of the college to furnish extensive psychiatric treatment to all students who need it." The primary role of the college psychiatrist is, therefore, not that of therapist. Then what is it? Farnsworth offers this answer:

> Much of the work of the school and college psychiatrists consists of crisis intervention. In such situations, it may not be clear who is the patient, or more frequently, there is no true patient nor can any person be assigned that role. Any time a teacher, administrator, or student is deeply troubled about the emotional reactions of someone to whom he has a responsibility, a talk with the college psychiatrist may be helpful.

We are thus told, first, that "there is no true patient"; second, that "any person may be assigned that role"; and third, that the college psychiatrist expects to have as his clients persons who do not themselves feel "troubled," but who wish to define others as "troubled" (indeed "deeply" so). Farnsworth speaks of unidentified X's who are "deeply troubled about the emotional reactions of" unspecified Y's. But we know perfectly well who these X's and Y's are. Administrators and faculty members have the privilege of incriminating students as mentally ill; students have the privilege of incriminating their fellow students as mentally ill; but students do not have the privilege of incriminating administrators and faculty members as mentally ill. In the social context of the school, as elsewhere, the role of (involuntary) mental patient is assigned to the low man on the totem pole. A further statement of Farnsworth's supports this inference:

> What the psychiatrist learns from the care of troubled students gives him the appropriate material for helping his colleagues in the academic disciplines to work more effectively with their students. When psychiatrists work in cooperation with deans and other faculty members on behalf of students, a great many people in the institutions become skilled in identifying, understanding and helping troubled students. If the college psychiatrist did not share his knowledge of the student in a general way with colleagues in other parts of the college or university, there would be no reason for his presence on the staff.

The roles are now allocated and the players defined. The student is *mentally sick* (he is "troubled"); the psychiatrist is supposedly a *therapist* (he "works on behalf of" the student); and the college faculty are *assistant therapists* (they will "work more effectively" with the student). But the college psychiatrist is a therapist in name only. His attitudes toward antisocial conduct and confidentiality define his role as that of policeman and judge.

> Library vandalism, cheating and plagiarism, stealing in the college and community stores or in the dormitories, unacceptable or antisocial sexual practices (overt homosexuality, exhibitionism, promiscuity), and the unwise and unregulated use of harmful drugs are examples of behavior that suggests the presence of emotionally unstable persons. . . .

Farnsworth is thus ready to regard the student who breaks laws or social customs as mentally ill and a fit subject for the attention of the college psychiatrist, whether the student wants such attention or not. This interpretation is supported by Farnsworth's statement that "those who steal from sheer perversity should be handled in one manner. Those who do so because of overwhelming emotional impulses should be referred for medical treatment." "Medical treatment" is here merely a euphemism for psychiatric control and punishment.

Moreover, how does Farnsworth, or any college psychiatrist, know whether or not students are guilty of these offenses? There is no mention of the student's rights, especially to be considered innocent until proven guilty.

The college psychiatrist appears to play one or both of two roles here. He is a police interrogator who induces the accused student to confess and incriminate himself, and then uses this information against him; or he is a judge who assumes that the student is guilty until proven

otherwise. In either case, he also assumes that such students are mentally sick until proven otherwise, and he
believes that his task is to divide these quasi-criminals
into two groups: those who break rules "from sheer perversity" and those who do so because of "illness."

Farnsworth speaks of students "who actively work out
their psychological problems in the library" (meaning that
they steal and mutilate books), and who send "threatening
communications . . . to department heads, deans, and
presidents. . . . [Since] the people who commit these acts
are usually disturbed, it is quite essential that they be
handled with respect for their disabilities and that punitive
attitudes be kept to a minimum." In plain English, Farnsworth prefers that deviant students be punished by means
of covert psychiatric sanctions rather than overt legal
sanctions.

A characteristic feature of the college psychiatrist's role
is its diffuseness and all-inclusiveness. This in turn leads
to commitments to contradictory goals. The main reason
for this is the psychiatrist's unwillingness to be restrained
by fixed rules—his insistence on his right to discretionary
behavior. Farnsworth frankly acknowledges this in another book on the subject:

The college psychiatrist has a dual responsibility which at
times puts him in a paradoxical situation. ... [He] is
obligated to treat students who have emotional conflicts
and to keep any information which they may give him in
complete confidence. He must also work with the administration to further mental health in the college in every
possible way. ... A constant alertness to the need for
keeping his various roles from becoming confused is a
necessary attitude on the part of any college psychiatrist.
Does the psychiatrist really take the role of impartial

mediator in disputes between a student and the administration? Farnsworth states on the one hand that "the
psychiatrist is not retained by the college to be an administrator or policeman"; but elsewhere he adds:

> When anti-social acts are involved, however, the psy-
> chiatrist must act on behalf of the university, and he
> must make this clear to the patient (though action that
> is directed to the best interests of the student will, of
> course, be best for the college or university).

Similar contradictions—or affirmations of mutually ex-
clusive goals and tasks—abound in the volume *Emotional
Problems of the Student,* edited by G. B. Blaine Jr. and C.
C. McArthur. For example, we read first that "the psychiatrist will want to talk with administrators and students with
a view toward the elimination of ... [psychiatric] excuses,"
and later that "except for cases where the student has been
caught by a coincidence of stresses, it should seldom be
recommended that he be excused from any academic demands." But elsewhere, Blaine frankly acknowledges that
"often professors want to know whether they can honestly
excuse a student because of his emotional illness, or a dean
may want to refrain from taking action if he knows that a
student is earnestly working in therapy." He considers such
requests "legitimate and necessary," from which we may
conclude that he supplies the information requested.

Here is another example of inconsistency: Blaine and
McArthur first declare that "the psychiatrist should not
have any authority for discipline. . . . If the psychiatrist
assumed functions of this kind, his capacity for objectivity
would be seriously impaired." But this statement is later
qualified so radically that its thrust is reversed:

> [There] are cases in which the personality structure of

the student, above and beyond his sexual deviation, makes him the cause of concern and discomfort for those about him and it is imperative that he leave the community. Here again, the psychiatrist's opinion in regard to the total personality picture is important in making the right disposition.

How and with whom does the college psychiatrist exchange information about student-patients, and how does he see the problem of confidentiality?

As Farnsworth noted, the college student is often not clearly identified as a patient. It follows, though he does not say this, that the psychiatrist's role is often similarly ill defined. Is he the student-patient's doctor, like a private physician? Or is he the institution's employee, like a physician who works for an insurance company? Here is Farnsworth's answer:

Although we would like to think that nothing of what goes on between patient and therapist in the privacy of an interview would ever have to be revealed to others, we know from our experience that such information about our student-patients can be very helpfully used at certain time of crises or decision. There are other situations in which our knowledge of how a student is behaving or thinking must be used to protect others in the community or the student himself. At such times general statements can be made to parents, faculty, or administrative officials after permission has been given by the student. In dangerous situations it must be transmitted, even if the student refuses permission, but only after he has been told that it will be done. On rare occasions, of course (such as when a homicidal patient rushes from the office before real communication has been established), there is no opportunity. . . .

General and specific information about students often must be given to deans and faculty at times other than during a weekly or bi-weekly conference, especially when prompt decisions are desirable. The usual rules of confidentiality must be upheld in such instances. Disciplinary action, postponements of academic obligations, such as examination papers or theses, and decisions about leaves of absence or withdrawals often depend upon recommendations or opinions given by a student's therapist.

What does Farnsworth mean when he says that "the usual rules of confidentiality must be upheld"? The word "upheld" seems almost like a misprint, for it is evident that the "usual rules of confidentiality" are here not upheld, but, on the contrary, are suspended. In any case, the college psychiatrist disperses information about his student-patient so widely as to make any reference to "confidentiality" absurd.

If the student is treated by a private therapist, the college psychiatrist may assume the role of intermediary, relaying information from the therapist to the administration. For example, when a student who has left school seeks readmission, Farnsworth suggests:

The evidence on which the college psychiatrist or director of the health service makes his decision [to recommend readmission or not] should include a full report from the psychiatrist who treated the patient while he was away (if any). . . . In doubtful cases, or when the evidence from the college psychiatrist and the impression of the private psychiatrist are at variance, it is probably kinder to postpone the student's re-entrance. . . .

Farnsworth thus recommends that the college psychiatrist

invade the student's private off-campus psychotherapy.

The relationship between college psychiatrist and student-patient is anything but confidential. And despite his own clear admission that, "if a psychiatric service is to enjoy the confidence of college presidents and trustees, some adequate channels of communication on matters not involving confidential physician-patient relations should be maintained between them," Farnsworth dismisses as a "rationalization" the students' "fear that confidences will not be maintained."

In the case of homosexuality, the college psychiatrist becomes an undisguised medical policeman: "The psychiatrist and the college police force must often work closely together, particularly in cases of homosexuality," says Farnsworth. Indeed, Farnsworth apparently views homosexuality as so grave a sin that the individual who commits it forfeits his rights to psychiatric privacy:

> When an administrator or a faculty member has referred a patient with a homosexual problem, the psychiatrist's report should simply state that the patient has consulted him, that treatment was (or was not) recommended, and that the psychiatrist will take appropriate action if the community and/or the patient requires it. This should be done orally in most instances, and even this exchange should remain confidential unless the patient indulges in further unacceptable social behavior.

The qualifying "unless" in the last sentence justifies the physician's betrayal of his patient's confidences precisely when it will injure him most. If the patient refrains from homosexual relations or lies about them, the psychiatrist has no damaging confidential information to protect; however, if he does engage in such conduct and confides it to his therapist, then the psychiatrist feels justified in reporting him to the authorities.

In this connection, Farnsworth strongly supports the principle and practice of coerced psychiatric treatment as a method of social control:

> The psychiatrist must convince the administration that homosexuality is a medical problem that can be successfully treated in some cases, whereas in others, the involved person can adapt without promiscuity or preying on young men with inevitable and tragic results. If, on the other hand, the homosexual is an active proselytizing undergraduate, treatment must be required.

Saying that homosexuality on the college campus is a medical problem does not make it so. Nor can I agree that Farnsworth's recommendation that the proselytizing homosexual, but not the proselytizing heterosexual, should be coerced to submit to psychiatric treatment is based on medical—instead of on moral and social—criteria. Nor, finally, do I believe that the kind of psychotherapy which Farnsworth advocates is described correctly by asserting that "the counseling we are discussing here is definitely not guidance in the sense of attempting to influence the student to go along some predetermined channel."

Blaine adheres to the same policy regarding the release of information about patients with homosexual problems. He writes in a journal article:

> An FBI agent calls to discuss a former patient and has a signed release from the student who is now applying for a responsible government position. While in college, this boy had sought help for homosexual preoccupation. He had engaged in homosexual activity in high school and once in college. The FBI agent wants to know if

the student had engaged in homosexual practices.

Here, at last, is an easy problem. The student is no longer in school. The FBI is not a part of the college's administrative structure. So why should the psychiatrist divulge information to the FBI?

Why? Because refusal to cooperate would be unpatriotic. "This is a difficult problem," says Blaine, "one involving loyalty to patients and to country." The college psychiatrist never seems content to serve but one master. If there is no conflict between student and school, he creates one between citizen and country. "We have found," continues Blaine, "that questions about homosexual practices usually can be answered in context without jeopardizing security clearance. Pointing out that an individual was going through a phase of development which involved him in temporary homosexual preoccupation and even activity does not seem to alarm these investigators."

Why, indeed, should it? They came looking for a homosexual, and they found him. Surely it is significant that, in all their voluminous writings on college mental health, Farnsworth and Blaine never suggest that the school psychiatrist should assist the student-patient's private lawyer or an attorney in the local chapter of the American Civil Liberties Union. Are we, then, asked to believe that the college psychiatrist "cooperates" with teachers, deans, the campus police, and the FBI in order to help the student, but never with lawyers who might protect his legal rights, because that would *not help* the student?

The far-reaching degree to which the psychiatrist's essential responsibility for keeping his patient's confidences is compromised is illustrated by the following observation of Farnsworth's, from his book *Mental Health in College and University*:

[One] of the most delicate problems that confronts a college psychiatrist is that of preserving the confidential nature of the physician-patient relationship. . . . Nothing that the patient divulges during the course of the medical interview may be used by the physician without the patient's permission, unless the welfare of others is directly at stake.

This is a remarkable modification of the Hippocratic code. Since it is easy to construe the conflicts and communications of psychiatric patients as threatening the welfare of others—particularly because "welfare" is undefined—Farnsworth's rule effectively nullifies the physician's pledge of confidentiality. Farnsworth is plainly aware that the college administration, which pays the psychiatrist, would not tolerate being left in the dark about students:

From the standpoint of the dean or faculty member who referred the student to the psychiatrist, the problem of confidence is not so clear-cut as is implied previously. If he calls the psychiatrist, asks about the student, and is told that the confidential patient-physician relationship prevents any comment, he is not going to be very happy about the situation.

But if a troubled student consulted his clergyman and lawyer, would they divulge his confession or confidence to keep the dean "happy"? Does this mean that clergymen and lawyers are less "responsible" toward the college or the community than psychiatrists? Or does it mean that they have more successfully resisted compromising the integrity of their roles?

My complete disagreement with the principles and practices of college psychiatry just outlined may be supported on the following two grounds. The first is the ambiguity of the college psychiatrist's role. He misrepresents himself to the student; were he to represent himself correctly, his prestige and power would be greatly diminished. The second is his self-defined standard of conduct. He abjures contracts or clear restrictions on his powers; instead, by exalting discretionary judgments dictated by "therapeutic" needs, he exercises arbitrary control over the student-patient.

A layman cannot purport to be a physician; a policeman cannot induce a suspect to confide in him by promising to help him in court; an attorney cannot simultaneously play the roles of prosecutor and defense lawyer. But the college psychiatrist can and does engage in this kind of false representation. He claims to be a physician, but his work is nonmedical. He treats students, by what Blaine and McArthur call "environmental manipulation," for diseases that are metaphoric in nature and whose symptoms are stealing books from the library or ingesting drugs forbidden by law. He also claims to be the student's therapist and ally, but when conflicting pressures are brought on him, he is the student's adversary.

The college psychiatrist, writes Farnsworth, "must not allow himself to be trapped by both the traditional role of the physician and his natural compassion for suffering into overlooking the needs of the community." He suggests further that, like other physicians employed and paid by third parties, the psychiatrist is responsible to his employer, not his patient:

Medical examinations performed for a third party (as,

for example, a federal agency such as the Federal Aviation Agency or an insurance company) do entail the responsibility that the physician who performs the examination will divulge accurately and completely all information obtained. A physician can be held liable for negligent actions in the performance and completion of such examinations and reports.

But even such a commitment to his employer appears not to be binding on the college psychiatrist. According to Farnsworth:

He must not be excessively identified with either the administration or his patients, but must be completely identified with and believe in the goals of the educational process and feel that his special talents are necessary to it.

There is no such thing as an "educational process" in the abstract, however, but only educational goals and activities entertained and practiced by students and faculty. In pledging loyalty to such a vague abstraction, the psychiatrist actually promises nothing. Perhaps because of this Farnsworth recommends that the college psychiatrist "be particularly careful in the way he conducts himself. He must never judge patients or colleagues publicly in terms of right or wrong, must try to remain free of bigotry, and, above all, must not appear to prefer one type of patient to the exclusion of another."

This is an exaltation of deception, mystification, and self-concealment. For Farnsworth here recommends that the college psychiatrist hide his value judgments and therapeutic goals from faculty and students alike and that he pretend to a freedom from personal preferences and prejudices which in fact he does not possess. This deception is necessary, perhaps, because it is impossible to disabuse the public in general, and students in particular, of their deep-seated conviction that psychiatrists are unlike ordinary physicians—that they are disciplinarians, not doctors. For example, a recent study of the professions and public esteem showed "doctors" in first place, with 74 percent of those questioned expressing a "great deal of confidence" in them. Psychiatrists were listed separately, however, and they appeared in seventh place, with a "confidence score" of 57 percent, following the bankers, scientists, military leaders, educators, and corporation heads.

This relatively low psychiatric prestige may well be an unintended consequence of the strenuous efforts with which the profession has curried public favor. Trying to prove how "useful" he can be—to government, industry, religion, the schools, indeed, to any powerful institution or group— the psychiatrist has sacrificed his loyalty to the individual patient or client.

The political character of college psychiatry is an example, in an educational context, of the Rule of Man.

There are two basic principles that regulate social relations: status and contract. The family is a typical status relationship, whereas the economic bond between a buyer and seller is a typical contract relationship. Status relations are characteristically hierarchical, as in the relation between master and slave; the inferior member of such a pair has little or no power to restrain his more powerful partner. In contrast, contractual relations tend to be equalitarian, as in the relation between two businessmen; each member commands some power to compel the other to fulfill his promises.

The relation between student and school psychiatrist is devoid of all contractual guarantees. It is a status relationship in which the psychiatrist is the superior, and the student the inferior, member of the pair. To illustrate the political import of this arrangement, let us briefly review the condition necessary for individual liberty—a value which college psychiatrists claim to hold in high esteem. F. A. Hayek declares in his book *The Road to Serfdom:*

> Nothing distinguishes more clearly conditions in a free country from those in a country under arbitrary government than the observance in the former of the great principle known as the Rule of Law. Stripped of all technicalities, this means that government in all its actions is bound by rules fixed and announced beforehand —rules which make it possible to forsee with fair certainty how the authority will use its coercive powers in given circumstances and to plan one's individual affairs on the basis of this knowledge. . . . Within the known rules of the game the individual is free to pursue his personal ends and desires, certain that the powers of government will not be used deliberately to frustrate his efforts.

The opposite of this arrangement is a system in which every conflict of interest is decided "on its own merits," authority always acting "in the best interests" of the subjects.

The real enemy of the Rule of Law is therefore not lawlessness or anarchy, but rather the demand for benevolent discretion on the part of the authorities. For by the use of discretion it is possible to preserve the form of a contract, while discarding its substance. When lawlessness rules, men crave law and order; but when legalism rules through the Rule of Man, and the law deliberately leaves decisions to the discretion of authority, law and order are destroyed behind a cloak of "justice." In medical and psychiatric bureaucracies, rules of fair play are similarly sacrificed, not for a social "justice," but for mental "health."

The ambiguity of the college psychiatrist's role, the vagueness of his language, and the use of unregulated power in his ostensibly therapeutic interventions—all these qualify him as a powerful status figure wielding vast authority over the student. Like the totalitarian ruler, he speaks of liberty but refuses to provide the one indispensable condition for its existence—namely, restraint on his own power, guaranteed by enforceable contract.

The psychiatrist's job, Farnsworth states, "is to help individuals who suffer from emotional conflict in whatever ways he can." This is the perfect definition, and the unqualified approval, of the psychiatric version of the Rule of Man. The psychiatrist defines and determines who suffers from "emotional conflict" and what constitutes "help"; and he may use unlimited discretion in being "helpful" (from advising that teachers treat the student with leniency to recommending that he be expelled from school or committed to a mental hospital).

In sum, the college psychiatrist doubly misrepresents himself and his role—first, by claiming that his work is like that of the nonpsychiatric physician, when, in fact, he deals not with the diseases of a sick person but with the social problems of the college campus; and second, by implying that he is the agent, simultaneously, of the student-patient whose personal confidences he respects and of the school administration whose needs for social control he fulfills. In fact, he is a double agent, serving both parties in a conflict but owing real loyalty to neither.

Toward the students, the college psychiatrist shows one side of his Janus-like face: He is a compassionate counselor and therapist who promises to be a faithful conspirator with the student in his struggle for liberation from parent and educational authorities. Toward the institution and the outside world, he shows the other side of his face: He is a wise physician who will select and control students and inform about them as the needs of the school and the community require.

This is the kind of false representation of the college psychiatrist's role and function that, if practiced by the police, industry, or medical establishments, would be denounced by critics and condemned by the courts. The same deception practiced in the name of mental health has, however, so far escaped both public criticism and judicial prohibition.

October 1967

BOOKS ON PSYCHIATRY BY THE AUTHOR:

The Myth of Mental Illness (New York: Hoeber-Harper, 1961). A critical analysis of the origins, nature, and social uses of the concept of mental illness.

Law, Liberty, and Psychiatry (New York: The Macmillan Company, 1963). A review and documentation of legal mental-health practices that deprive people of civil rights.

The Ethics of Psychoanalysis (New York: Basic Books, 1965). A study of the psychoanalytic relationship as a human situation, rather than as a medical or therapeutic situation.

Student Power
In Action

ARLIE HOCHSCHILD

Cubans use the term "university revolution" to mean something different from the pickets and tear gas now its trade-
mark on American campuses. The Cuban revolution of
1958 turned the University of Havana on its head. Established faculties were dismantled. Professors left and were
replaced by students. Transformation of education took
place in the time that the University of California at
Berkeley spent publishing a report on what should be done
about its own troubled campus. Ironically, many recommendations made at Berkeley to establish a sense of community and better student-faculty relations are realities in
Cuba, an unintended result of more far-reaching political,
economic, and social upheaval. The 27,000 students of the
University of Havana complain not of impersonality, lack
of community, access to teachers, or the "irrelevance" of
what they learn, but of a lack of qualified teachers (three-
fourths of the chemistry faculty are students teaching
courses they have just passed) and a lack of textbooks in

their own language (due to a shortage of paper and of foreign exchange).

In some ways, student generations in the United States have their opposites in Cuba. The Cuban counterpart of the silent fifties on American campuses was an activist generation in which most of the 20,000 people killed by Batista's army and secret police were students.

What changes, then, has the revolution brought to this generation of Cuban students? How have the university reforms affected the individual student and his quest for a personal identity? How do Cuban and American students compare?

To understand the Cuban students of today we must compare them to the generation that went before. The University of Havana, the oldest and largest university in Cuba, was in the 1950's a prism of Cuba's turbulent political life and a training ground for its leaders. Student activists were waging more than a verbal war on the Batista regime from the campus citadel. Their protest showed that when governments are weak, students can be strong. As in the 1930's when students led the urban resistance to the Machado regime (during which the University was closed for three years), students of the 1950's were actively protesting against a government whose secret police terrorized the city and brought martyrdom, jail, or exile to thousands of students.

Students of the 1950's came to be called the Moncada generation after an abortive attack in 1953 on Batista's Moncada barracks in Oriente, led by Fidel Castro, a recent graduate of the law faculty of the University of Havana. Almost everyone you meet in that generation still in Cuba —now in their 30's and 40's—claims some credit for Batista's downfall, either indirectly, through a martyred brother or exiled friend, or directly, as part of the 26th of July movement, the May 1 movement, or the student-led 13th of March attack on the Presidential palace.

When the Moncada generation—now graduated and part of the establishment—took over, in their green fatigue uniforms, the management of hospitals, stores, farms, and factories, the spirit of top leaders and the paramilitary structure of the Party somehow kept the machinery running despite the fact that political loyalty counted more than training and skill in appointments to key jobs.

To its successors, the Moncada generation appears as a generation of doers and pragmatists—of active Quixotes rather than contemplative Hamlets.

The post-Moncada generation, now 18 to 25 years old, has taken a different role in Cuban history, not as destroyers of the old but as builders of the new. As children they watched and heard the revolution come to power, as adolescents they became its young assistants, and as university students they stepped into a newly reconstructed university. In the literacy campaign of 1961, 45,000 of these teenagers volunteered to live with peasant families for six to eight months, spreading the gospel of the revolution to the countryside and teaching basic literacy. (A is for *agricultura*, R is for *revolución* and so on.) They came to know the peasants for the first time not as passers of arms and food but as students and political converts. Predictably, the campaign taught the predominantly urban middle-class youngsters as much as it taught the peasants. One student recalled, "No one in the family I taught had been to school before; there were no schools close enough to walk or ride by horse to and return within a day . . . I slept in a hammock outside the hut, to avoid the insects. The father taught me how to kill snakes and drain them of oil. We used the oil in the lamp we read by in the evening. . . . I tried to explain to my family that the earth was round, but they insisted that it was flat. They knew the fields were flat." Many lessons were drawn from newspaper articles, and as another student later recounted, "I decided to explain to my family that Gagarin, the Russian astronaut had tried to reach the moon. They wouldn't believe me. I was too young to know. How could a man reach the moon? The moon is a virgin which no man may touch. . . ." The student went on, "I took them on their first trip to Havana. They were afraid to cross the street. They waited for four and a half hours for a bus because they didn't know where to look for the number of the bus."

If the literacy campaign was a cultural crusade against rural feudalism, it was also a training ground in self-sufficiency for its young teachers. It accustomed them to authority, to improvising solutions to unpredictable problems, and it forged a spiritual link to the Moncada generation. Although no student mentioned this, the experience might also have made them less envious of the great comforts of the urban upper class toward which they were oriented. At the same time, it probably made them thankful for the urban comforts they did have, comforts conspicuously absent from peasant life.

The post-Moncada generation, like the generation before it, has lived a period of history which "deprivatized" them by putting a public revolutionary claim on their private lives. Their future does not, as Kenneth Keniston says of alienated American youth, "inspire scant enthusiasm." It is not the dread thing it appeared to be to the soft-faced "graduate" (in the film) standing inert on an automatic conveyor belt in a Los Angeles airport. The airports of Cuba have few enough planes and parts and pilots, let alone conveyor belts for passengers. For Cuban students before and after the revolution, the task at hand—to end a reign of terror and to move from the idea of a virgin moon to the idea of an astronaut—demands a kind of dedication that would appeal to what Erik Erikson calls "the ideological mind" that marks the period of the "identity crisis." The melding of private ambitions into public goals—the impulse to be part of something larger that sends American youth into Freedom Summers, SDS projects, or the Peace

Corps (to put them all in the same bag)—is the same desire that responds to national demands on the young *sabras* of Cuba.

But beyond that, personal identity seems to have for many in both generations of Cuban students a deeper political dimension. The thousand Cubans a week who renounce their citizenship, and the Voice of America from Miami, are constant reminders of an implicit choice. For those who choose to remain, to be Cuban is, to quote a favorite phrase in revolutionary rhetoric, "to be integrated into the revolution." There are strong social pressures to actively participate in national programs, to spend spare time cutting cane or planting coffee. Militia duty for both men and women students is now compulsory. Behind the willingness of students to respond to these pressures is a mood created by events such as the Bay of Pigs invasion, a sense of immediacy about the threat to the Castro regime that wars in foreign places can seldom match. For the mainstream of American youth, the fate of the nation is, by contrast, more remote and the link between self and nation less direct.

Young people in Cuba, more than their American counterparts, are celebrated as a "chosen people." There are plaques and billboards throughout towns and villages bearing the names of young patriotic martyrs of bygone struggles; political rhetoric dates the birth of the country itself to the revolution and a majority of those in positions of power in Cuba are under 30. As Gilda Betancourt, the 25-year-old chairman of the sociology department at the University of Havana, explained, "You have to be young to take all the changes. Last month I went out to cut cane for a month and when I came back, my office had been changed, new programs had been proposed, old plans discarded. It was hard getting back to my old daily pattern. It would be almost impossible if I were 50."

Their ability to act as a shock absorber of change, their

willingness to innovate, to be ideologically committed, make the youth a ready and trusted workforce to replace those whose commitments, if not their training, are outmoded. The complaints of the young are not that they are denied adulthood but that they are hurried into it, that they have "never been young." Indeed they look with some envy at the new, more leisured generation—now 14 to 18 —who conceal skin-tight. jeans under their baggy, tan school uniforms.

The situation is otherwise for American youth who are, by contrast, worshipped but not honored. They are supposed to "enjoy the best years of their lives" but remain, like the ladylove of the chivalrous knight, functionless on the pedestal.

While the Moncada and post-Moncada generations share characteristics which distinguish them from American students, the post-Moncada generation differs spiritually if not politically from its predecessor. The post-Moncada generation is critical of the puritanical intolerance of ideological or sexual deviance that characterizes the revolutionary Moncada generation. (Homosexuals are barred from the Party and a talented writer in the Faculty of Letters was discharged from the University for being an open homosexual.) A Moncada fighter, who now sits in an office and assigns scholarships to students, is notorious among students for withholding money from girls known to have slept with their boyfriends. Cuba does not import the pill.

Although this may not be a general difference, my impression is that the younger generation has more of a sense of humor about the revolution and its rhetoric than do their elders. The newspapers, radio, and posters advertise the notion of moral rather than material incentives for work. A young poet described doing productive labor (voluntary agricultural work) one weekend in the company of some older party functionnaires. As they sliced along the rows of sugar cane, he playfully remarked to his neighbor,

"Since the price of sugar is only 2 cents on the world market, why don't we import rather than export sugar? That way we can save money and stop work." The man stared at him blankly, then patiently began to explain why Cuba had to export sugar, much to the young poet's dismay.

Just as a generation of protest gave way to a generation of acceptance, so the university, once a citadel of revolt, is now "integrated into the revolution." The education it offers points students to the task of putting the Economic Plan into effect—off of paper and into goods and services.

The university has been retailored to make useful quasi-generalists of doctors, economists, architects, chemists, engineers, teachers, and dentists—to breed a new model of man for whom academic and vocational life, intellect and action, national, group, and individual loyalties are more integrated.

But the gains were also losses. The revolution which divided the student generations also divided opinion about the university. To faculty and students who wanted a center of humanistic learning, free of government control, the reforms that began in 1959 were a disaster. The concept of a community of scholars dedicated to the search for truth and to training for the liberal professions went out with the revolution when the university lost the fragile autonomy it once had. Four of the largest faculties—medicine, engineering, architecture, and law—collectively refused to accept the authority of the *Federactión Estudiantil Universitaria* (which claims that university autonomy was being used for counterrevolutionary ends) and resigned.

Today, a growing minority of students compete for and are selected into the Young Communist organization: Journalism and political science have the highest proportion of members, but 900 of 4,000 students in the technology faculty also belong. The criteria for membership bear on all aspects of life—revolutionary dedication, moral uprightness, and good grades. But once accepted by the Party, the threat of withdrawal can result in repression: One student was "separated" (as opposed to expelled) from the YC because she planned to take up art as well as the more useful vocation of medicine.

On the other hand, those who support the reforms say that the university has put into effect priorities for university resources more in line with the needs of Cuba's underdeveloped economy. Before the revolution the university was out of touch with economic realities. Between 1925 and 1930 the University graduated 2,830 students among whom were only eight electrical engineers, one agricultural engineer, and 12 sugar engineers. Eight hundred and ninety-one students graduated in law.

As Castro asked in a speech, "Do you know how many (students) have been trying to enter the diplomatic service at the University of Havana? Three thousand students. And do you know how many wanted to study economics? Not even one hundred!"

Since 1960 the University of Havana and its two offspring, the University of Las Villas (4,000 students) and Oriente (5,300 students), have become vocational training centers. Its former three faculties (law, medicine, and letters and arts) have grown to eight: technology, agronomy, medicine, sciences, teaching, economy, humanities, and the workers and peasant faculty—an adult extension division which prepares its 4,000 lower-class students to enter one of the other seven faculties, usually technology or agriculture. The most important of these and the largest is the 30-million-dollar new Faculty of Technology (the *Ciudad Universitaria*), which enrolls 4,000 students, over half of whom are on complete scholarships.

For all students, textbooks are free at any bookstore, many of which are stocked with medical and technical tomes written in English and printed offset by the Cuban Book Institute, in defiance of international copyright laws.

The experiment with priorities has put every field of learning into a state of constant flux. One recent graduate in arts from the University of Oriente complained, "The first year they told us that we would learn linguistics when we specialize, after we got a foundation. The second year they told us that linguistics *was* the foundation." Students having to repeat a second-year course found that it was not the *same* second-year course that they had previously flunked.

According to the vice-rector of the University of Havana, "The university is not designed to develop specialists. It is designed to develop useful people." (After a two-hour interview, the vice-rector, who was also a professor of medicine and a practicing doctor, excused himself because he had to perform an operation.) These changes toward pragmatism have meant that technology students become people who can run factories, not researchers. For doctors, it means more who can vaccinate children, fewer who can transplant organs. For economists, it means more general consultants and planners and fewer specialists in particular fields (and no private businessmen). This does not mean the elimination of specialization, but a reduction of it, as the needs of rural areas are met.

Pure research, though minimal, is not absent from the new priorities, and all research has been turned over to the National Center of Scientific Research and the Academy of Sciences. Professors are promoted by student-faculty committees on the basis of ability to teach and "revolutionary commitment," rather than on research.

Like small American colleges, there is little social distance between teacher and student. In some cases the same person is formally both. The mass exodus of professors at the time of the revolution and again in 1960 left the university bereft of its most precious resource. According to the vice-rector of the University, all but 13 of some 300 medical professors left, and that was typical of other faculties. As a stopgap measure, recent graduates and top students in their last years have been appointed to the faculty. Sixty percent of the faculty of technology in 1968 were either recent graduates or undergraduates in their fourth or fifth year. The psychology department had four faculty members with the equivalent of a Ph.D., and the chemistry department had one. A Cuban report to UNESCO showed "teaching personnel" at the University of Havana as 2,222 in the beginning of 1965 and 3,017 in the beginning of 1966; most of the additions were students.

If the lines of authority within the university are blurred, it is partly because professors and students see each other in so many different contexts. Almost every field of training—called a *carrera*—has a program of "preprofessional work" that sends professor and student out into the field together, for anywhere from two weeks to two months a year.

"Preprofessional work" orients the student toward a vocation, and gives him a basis for "relevance" in his academic studies, just as the correspondence courses after graduation suggest the relevance of academic studies to his vocation. Like the system of "productive labor" (voluntary agricultural or factory work), it shows him what needs to be done, and gives him some idea of where he could do his two years of social service, which are now compulsory for all university graduates.

The blend of classroom and field work is different for each university, each faculty, and each school. But in one way or another, each school divides its students into small groups called *equipos,* which work together in the countryside at something deemed educative and also economically (and in some cases politically) useful. Last year students in construction engineering joined a team of engineers who were building roads in Camaguey Province. An *equipo* of chemical engineers worked in a fertilizer factory, talking to workers and analyzing the products at various stages of production. Medical students vaccinated sugar-cane cutters, and dentistry students examined the teeth of peasants. Students in geography analyzed soils of different regions. Law students participated in "people's courts" in the Isle of Pines.

One *equipo* of about 33 economics students devised new production methods in a grapefruit juice factory in the Isle of Pines and wrote a report both for their university requirement and for the National Institute of Agrarian Reform, the introduction and conclusion of which was required reading for all other economics students. (Calculations were made on the university computer.) At the same time the office staff in the factory had a hand in the report and was taught how to plan by the economics students. The students, who in their first, second, and third year had read Keynes and Samuelson as well as Marx, were arguing about the applications of Frederick Taylor to the division of labor in the grapefruit juice factory, and had concluded that too much division of labor would harm worker morale. Their plan called for rotating workers—so that everyone could have a hand at all the kinds of work (mostly semiskilled)—and for monthly meetings to "orient" (which has the connotation of "explain" or "tell") the workers about the relation of little tasks to the whole plan.

Half of the 62 students in their third year of journalism do their preprofessional training by running *El Mundo,* one of Havana's two metropolitan daily newspapers. Its editor, a 27-year-old newspaperman, said that "graduates will go to provincial newspapers, though some may want to send an article or two from the field. They like it. Last year they visited newspapers and did a study of how people read a newspaper, but they like running the paper better. They learn more."

In the afternoon and evening, some of the five part-time teachers supervise students who make up various sections of the newspapers. In the morning, classes are held in the office and the faults in yesterday's front page are inspected and discussed. The conflict between the demands of training journalists, which requires rotation of personnel, and the demands of getting the paper to press on time has resulted in a series of snags. A student may be just getting the feel of the European news section when he is switched to sports, which he knows little about. There is also the problem of staggering student vacations so that enough students will be continually working on the paper. One journalism student commented, "It was chaos at first. But we know that we have a lot of readers and we have to learn fast. It's exciting, I didn't know whether I wanted to be a journalist before when we just visited newspapers; running one has helped me decide to be a journalist."

For this journalism student, the irrelevance of his education was not a complaint. And for most university students a vocation was something they practiced more than wondered about.

Preprofessional work in all fields integrates the postrevolution generation of students into the economic experiments of their elders, an experience which both the Moncada generation in Cuba and American students could only privately improvise, or for various reasons would resist. The educational system seems to curb the growth of political or hippie or collegiate subcultures within the university walls and to discourage the nonstudent fringe by the educational hurdles between them and an interesting job. Just as people living under food rations learn the virtue of thrift, so students who balk at the"irrelevance" of their education are considered a luxury the revolution cannot afford.

While the relevance of education is not an issue to this generation of Cuban students, they do object to being railroaded into careers that are of little interest to them but are of high priority to the state. Most agree that the needs of the revolution ought to be filled within the parameters of one's own personal needs, interests, and talents, except in times of political crisis—although sometimes students disagree about what constitutes a crisis and whether Cuba is in one now.

According to Paul Goodman, a youth seeks his identity in the "nether-netherland" between what he likes to do, what he is good at, and what needs doing. If what needs doing is determined in a capitalist country by the market, it is determined in a socialist country such as Cuba by the Economic Plan.

The notion of "the integrated man" which underlies higher education in Cuba is also behind the program of voluntary "productive labor," which sends students to one of the University's 11 farms for a weekend a month and one month in the summer.

I worked on one University farm in the cordon, or greenbelt, which circles Havana, in which 70 or so of the 280 students in Letters from the humanities faculty collectively do their stint. An ambitious six-year plan had designated the land, formerly a hog farm, to be converted into a botanical garden harboring every major species of plant in the tropical world. Greatly lacking the latest technology, the men students used an ox to draw their cart when the tractor broke down—which it often did—and the women were planting little pieces of grass in tin cans to make a mall which might have been more efficiently done with lawn seed had that been available.

In addition to the students there were 20 professors and the janitor from the University, all of whom worked and lived together in the men's or women's barracks on the farm. Paid day laborers and a group of prospective emigrants, who must work for at least three months in order to leave the country, worked on the farm and commuted home to Havana in the evening. Work began at 7:00 and continued until 5:00 at a steady if not arduous pace, with a short break at 10:00 and the traditional two-hour lunch and siesta break.

As they bent over the cans, with the sound of rifle practice in the distance, students sang nursery rhymes in Latin —there was a favorite Latin teacher in the group—and American pop songs including "San Francisco," "My Little Darling," from the 1950's, and all the Beatles' songs. They regaled each other with anti-Chinese jokes and discussed divorced friends; there have been many divorces since the revolution. They talked about the housing shortage in Havana; some married couples lived with their parents while waiting for their name to come up on the university housing list. They occasionally played a "guess who I'm thinking about" game where yes and no answers led the group to a name someone had in mind; the name was often that of an American movie star who played in movies ten years ago (no American films have been shown in Cuba since the embargo on American goods), although one Russian professor who had studied six years in the Soviet Union always named Soviet artists and scientists unknown to the group. No Chinese name came up while I was there.

Finally in the evening after work, groups of students huddled in circles outside the barracks around a tiny kerosene heater that held a tiny pot of precious, rationed coffee brought from various homes. The tin cup of coffee went ceremoniously around the circle until it was gone, and the students argued about the Bolivian minister of Interior who had given Che Guevera's diary to Castro. They sang Beatles' songs and sentimental Spanish songs in an exaggerated warble on into the night.

Living together and sharing common deprivations, tasks, and aims resulted in a natural communal spirit. They didn't talk about or contrive community; with all its advantages and disadvantages, they had it.

The post-Moncada generation tend to be culturally oriented toward the North, politically to the South. They tend to talk of coffee rather than community, of integration into the revolution rather than cooptation by it, of the practicalities of their vocation, rather than "irrelevance" of what they learn, of political loyalty and technical knowhow, rather than of College Board scores and Graduate Record exams, of the needs of the revolution rather than personal ambitions, of a teacher's good and bad points rather than his remoteness, and of responsibilities rather than—in spite of the legacy—protest.

The third generation of Cuban youth, now in their teens, as the benefactor of the revolution, has what the post-Moncada generation in grandfatherly tones call a "safe, comfortable life." They are given free schooling, free meals, board, and books. The revolutionary heroism is someone else's story, a source of vicarious pride. Their battle is the more mundane one of loosening parental constraints and shaping a life in which miniskirts or long hair are not a revolutionary sin. It is hard to know how many high-school students are trying to be ordinary teenagers, but the second generation goes along with school measures that remind the young of the hard life, the debt. The post-Moncada generation echoes the Party's hope that the toughness and youth of the country will become its permanent feature, that each generation will, as the saying goes, "give the flag" to the next, but countries, like individuals, do not remain young: The flag changes meaning, and what it is to be young changes with history.

Cuban youth, like Cuba itself, should rightfully be compared to the pre-revolutionary generation in Cuba or to present Bolivian, Chilean, or Israeli youth, not to American or French youth. But there is some use in comparing them to the youth of postindustrial countries such as the United States because of the light it sheds on American students and their search for personal identity. Different societies put different burdens on the answers to the questions: "who am I, what shall I be, what shall I do?" American youth are less integrated into the social and political life of their country, and life is less harsh than in Cuba. They are

socially kept young longer and get older without becoming
adult. The country itself is taking only what might be
called an "identity check-up." Cuban youth, by contrast,
are if anything *too* integrated into the social, economic,
and political life of their country. They are given adulthood
without demanding it. They can readily identify with the
generation of young heroes, Che, its martyred saint and
Fidel, its St. Peter, that went before and now hold power, a
generation which has improvised an educational system
that beckons them, honors them, pays for them, mobilizes
them, and rewards them with positions of responsibility
and authority. It also politicizes them, militarizes them, and
restricts them as the family and Church did before.

Consequently, what sense of indecision does characterize
Cuban adolescents does not in itself distinguish them from
their elders in power. If in any society it is a minority who
experience an identity crisis, in Cuba the minority is smaller. The term *identity crisis* is as inflated when applied to
Cuban youth as the term *revolution* is when applied to
American universities. The identity crisis, itself born of the
"psychosocial moratorium on adulthood" is like the hippie
movement, another luxury of a complex and affluent society which a revolution in earnest does without.

April 1969

POSTSCRIPT:

This article is not based on a systematic survey but on a series of
in-depth interviews with students, faculty and administrators of
the University of Havana. Besides Jose Yglesias' "Cuba Report:
Their Hippies, Their Squares" (The New York Times Magazine,
January 12, 1968) and Wassily Leontief's "Notes on a Visit to
Cuba," (The New York Review of Books, August 21, 1969)
there have been no published articles on Cuban student life in
the late sixties. The experimental nature of Cuban social
engineering makes writing about it risky. Descriptions of
particular projects are as quickly outdated as the projects
themselves. For example, the project of training journalists at
El Mundo, one of Havana's two major newspapers, was stopped in

1969 when the newspaper itself folded due to the paper shortage.

Note on University Life:

For a description of university life before the revolution see
Andres Suarez, *Cuba: Castroism and Communism 1959-1966,*
(Cambridge: MIT Press, 1967). As Suarez points out, the
students who returned from prison or exile after Machado's
downfall in 1933 took virtual control of the university, with the
good wishes of the "revolutionary" government then in power,
thus setting a partial precedent for the events of the sixties.
Ironically, an American Foreign Policy Commission, writing in
1935, noted that the majority of university students "were older by
three years than subsequent student groups will be, and matured by
the responsibilities and activities of three years of revolution, an
experience through which no other generation of students should
have to pass." *Problems of the New Cuba: Report of the
Commission on Cuban Affairs* (New York: Foreign Policy
Association, Inc., 1935, p. 154).

The university under the impact of the revolution is described
by Luis Boza Dominquez, an émigré professor, in *La Situacion
Universitaria en Cuba* (Editorial Del Pacifico, 1962). It is also
touched on in Theodore Draper's *Castro's Revolution: Myths and
Realities* (New York: Praeger, 1962, esp. p. 14). Also see
Enrique Gonzales Pedrere, *La Revolucion Cubana,* (Mexico:
Universidad Nacional Autonomía de Mexico, 1959); Pedro Vicente
Aja, "La Crisis de la Universidad de La Habana," *Guadernos,*
no. 47, March-April 1961, pp. 18-25; Carlos Rafael Rodriquez,
"La Reforma Universitaria," in *Cuba Socialista,* February, 1962,
pp. 22-44, which portrays the university reforms as an offshoot
of the "Moviemento de Cordoba" in Argentina in 1918. For the
impact of political events on generations see Maurice Zeitlin,
Revolutionary Politics and the Cuban Working Class, chapter 9,
"Political Generations" (Princeton, New Jersey: Princeton
University Press, 1967) and Karl Mannheim, *Essays on the
Sociology of Knowledge,* chapter 7, "The Problem of Generations"
(Paul Keckskemeti, editor, New York: Oxford University Press,
1952). Orthodox Marxists in Cuba do not concede any conflict
other than class conflict, but the issue of generational conflict
among Cuban intellectuals was publicly debated in *La Gaceta
de Cuba* (April-May 1966).

Note on Political Organization:

Few sources deal with political organization in the university since the revolution. In 1955 there were 26 communists (seven cells) in the university (See Suarez, ibid, p. 7). In 1968, according to the general secretary of the Young Communists in the Faculty of Technology, there were 900 party members out of 4000 students. Each July 26th, students nominated for Vanguardia are voted on by the entire student body. Vanguardia members are eligible to join the Young Communists; every year from 50 to 150 Vanguardia members join the ranks of the Young Communists.

Note on the "New Man":

One of the aims of the Party is to create "the New Man" who responds to moral and not material incentives, who enjoys his work and who puts the claims of the revolution above private ambition. More precisely, the new man does not put the claims of the revolution *above* private ambition; his private ambition is not at odds with his social obligations and he wants to do what he has to do.

The academic version of the "New Man" is being trained by the C.N.I.C., set up in 1964. The 200 graduate students now in training will teach later in the university and, according to the vice-rector of the University of Havana, the policy is to avoid a narrow scientific orientation, and to develop generalists and well-rounded people. E. N. Eisenstadt notes the stress, among Israeli youth, on a well-rounded personality, not limited by occupational blinders. (*From Generation to Generation,* New York: Free Press, 1956, p. 236.) While the image of the "New Man" serves, as Eisenstadt points out, to accentuate the differences between the generations, Cubans are trying to change the old men too. Of course many of the older generation have left Cuba. (At the time of the revolution, those faculty members who left the university were Cuban since the law at that time forbade employing foreign professors. Today there are about a hundred foreign professors, mainly in technological fields.)

Note on Attitude toward American Youth:

Cuban students are generally intrigued with the hippie subculture in the United States. They associate it with drugs (which went out with the revolution) and Beatles music. (A Beatles record underarm is a status symbol. They somehow manage to erase music from records imported before 1958 and re-record Beatles music.) However, they also consider the hippie movement a bourgeois perversion of the image of the "New Man" and see the hippies as the "children of the empire at play." The interest in, but lack of identification with hippies, is no accident; despite the primitive communism of some hippie groups, the present generation of Cubans could not be more different. It is as integrated into its society, as oriented toward the future and vocational life, as hard working, thrifty and extroverted as the hippies are opposed to their society, present-oriented, leisured and introspective.

For example, the hippie interest in astrology only amuses or bewilders the Cuban revolutionary whose task is to uproot traditional "superstition" among the peasantry. Differences between the two groups extend even to the *modes* of ego diffusion which, according to Erikson, characterize the unsuccessful quest for identity. If hippies or hippie-sympathizers sometimes deny or avoid the question of identity through passive observation of their "inner forces," Cuban revolutionaries seem to dismiss the same question by an acquiescence, equally passive, to the outer dictates of the economic plan.